Ecstasy & Her Blues

Kiana Nicole

Cover Art by SixAboveStudios

Find Kiana on Twitter @MISSKIANANICOL3

Find Kiana On Instagram @Missecstasy

Table Of Contents

What A Time To Be Alive

Dreams & Nightmares

Rhythm & Blues

The Culture

Butterflies

The Last Songs

Introduction

I'm so glad you made it here.

I have so much to tell you and I hope on this journey

through Ecstasy & Her Blues, you find yourself, too.

You're here right now for a reason.

In this book, you will find the purpose.

Whatever that may be for you.

With each chapter, brings a new enlightenment

towards topics such as adolescence coming of age,

dreams and nightmares of society, the human culture,

embracing both masculine and feminine energies,

the battle with mental health, spirituality, heartbreak, healing

and last but not least, the greatest moments of life and love.

So allow yourself to tune all the way in and enjoy the ride.

All based on a true story.

Here is my heart.

What A time To Be Alive

∞

My muse behind these words
I have promised you my love until the end of time
and with that you shall live forever.
For I have given you immortality.
Here is where you shall live for eternity...

TBH

Everything is nothing
how I pictured them a year ago.
I'm still trying to find my way,
I'm still trying to keep going day by day,
I'm still trying to hold my balance,
and be okay with accepting and understanding
that everything gets recycled,
and things come and go on their own timing.
I'm not sure if I'm being taught to let go more frequently,
or if the lesson is to watch things return home inevitably.
I should just go with the frequency.
Something tells me I'm going to lose way more than I expected
before I win.
Maybe I should quit expecting,
and quit smoking and stop that drinking.
Cause I can't focus,
Overthinking.
Some things are really out of my control.
So I've been letting God handle all things above me.
Asking God "Do you hear me now?"
No, I don't hear a sound.
But I'll see you around.
You always find a way to show up for me
and I promise you won't be missed...I see you

Honestly, I've been brokenhearted for as long as I could remember.
But you could never tell because I wear it well.
I know you probably feel empty,
and all out of energy to get out of bed in the mornings.
I know every day feels like war,
I know how you shield your heart not wanting to feel pain no more,
I know when you cry it pours,
I know how you feel...misunderstood.
I also know that better days are yet to come.
You must go through the storm to see the sun.
This life is our grandest adventure.
We must love every moment even the struggle days.
Rid yourself of toxicity and anything standing in your way.
Let go of your past life, you don't live there no more.
Trust and believe you are exactly where you need to be.
Now create a legacy
to carry on to infinity and beyond.
Look at yourself in the mirror even when you don't recognize who you are
and remember... you are the architect of your own life.

Legend In Me

We dreamed about this life.
Convos about condos, driving foreign cars
and clothes we can't pronounce.
Insomniac nights, putting up a fight, 9-5 ain't for life.
Had to hustle just to make things right.
I have a vision I must pursue to make dreams come true.
I paved this path of my own.
Mark my words, it's set in stone.
This road isn't easy, I had to make sacrifices along the way.
All for the family to eat
and my baby could see a better day.
I'm not your typical schoolgirl, that life don't belong to me.
Here where I'm at, this is my everything.
I came up from nothing, I knew I had to be something.
Even if that means me being the only one who believes in me.
My blessings are on the way.
I remember I prayed for this day.
To be here right now is a blessing on it's own.
Told myself if I want it I'm going to get it
even if that means doing it alone.
On my way to the top and nobody is really understanding me.
If you aren't here while I'm building,
don't come around later and act like you're my family.
I want to see you win and I want to see you eat.
Just not with me if you don't support my dreams.
My table is reserved for those who see the legend in me.

The Artist

Lovely blue inked fingers.
A collection of the unmentionable.
The universal truth.
A craftsman in the boondocks
creating a place to escape and call home.

Don't Play 17 Again

I find myself still praying for better days.
I find myself going out on Friday nights all for a quick thrill
and other times I find myself in my own pity party in my bedroom
because I haven't done enough work to celebrate.
I've been trying to convince myself that it's all worth it.
Even when I feel completely hopeless,
hoping nobody notices that none of this feels right anymore.
So I hide myself, away from the world.
I just don't have the energy for anything.
So I'll apologize a million times
and forgive myself all in the same breath.
I'm just still trying to find me.
Sometimes I retrace my steps back to the girl I once was
because she always feels like home.
Maybe because she's all I ever known.
Maybe she's my bad habit
because I still have a hard time
accepting that I don't live there anymore.
Somehow the girl I used to be and the woman I'm becoming
is in conflict with each other.
Maybe the lesson I need to face
is that I've graduated from the old me.
Now it's time I reinvent a new home.
Maybe then I'll recognize myself again.
The woman I'm meant to be --
But not until I let her go.

It's time I let her go so
she can find her way in the world.
So she can grow into the woman
that the little girl inside of her can be proud of.
So she can write her wrongs and turn them into beautiful songs.
I'm sorry I held you for so long. I shouldn't have kept you hidden.
But you found a way to build yourself out of that bedroom
covered in magazine posters
of other woman you always dreamed to be like.
I always knew you had it in you. If only you listened to yourself.
I'm still trying to love what I hear when I listen to myself.
I'm still trying to accept that the truth
isn't always what you want to hear
because the truth isn't always pretty, my dear.
Now realizing maybe it was fear that kept me away for so long.
Fear of letting go, fear of starting new again.
Because little did I know,
I had everything I ever wanted waiting for me on the other side.
Waiting for me to realize that what I've been holding onto
is causing me all this pain and confusion.
I've been blocking my own blessings.
But it's only a matter of time until I can thoroughly say...
I'm ready to be through with this.
I'm ready to meet the woman waiting for me on the other side.

Lust For Life & Live For Love

Why are you really mad?
What makes you really sad?
Are you allowing other people to control you?
By letting them trigger your emotions?
Your bitterness will always be unpleasant and distasteful.
There's no need for the green in you to act out of character.
Humble your being.
No need for revenge, let karma do her thing.
What do you get out of being mean?
What do you get out of doing things out of spite?
Do you believe that'll take you to higher heights?
What are you jealous of?
Who or what do you wish was yours?
What is it that you want more of?
If you just sit for a moment and appreciate all that you have,
you'll have an abundance.
If you change your mindset into thinking
'nobody is better than me,
and I am capable of achieving the same,
if not greater level of greatness as the people whom I idolize
You'll kill not only your comparisons, but fear.
We have a choice here.

Because at the start of every day,
we all have the same 24 hours.
Don't let another human,
who bleeds just like you discourage you.
Don't let authority belittle you.
Don't let nobody tell you what you can and cannot do.
Don't fall victim like a fool.
It's all up to you to choose what you will do for the day.
That'll take you a step further to achieving your goals.
When you come to an understanding
that you have a choice to be who you want,
I hope you choose to be great.
I hope you choose to lust for life and live for love.

Viva La Vida

You know, you only live one.
So I hope you're living your best life.
Like, doing whatever the fuck you want.
Whatever to keep your spirit high.
Find a drive
Don't get caught in traffic
Stay on the move
Even with no destination
Just drive
You'll find a way
Just ride
Along the way you'll find
Your way in life
Take your time
Enjoy the ride...

Astral World Trip

I feel electric and alive.
The light is beaming,
The birds are singing,
The bells are ringing,
The rose awakening,
Rebel flower, they're calling you.
Geometric patterns leading to the astral realms.
I discovered something beyond me.
I feel it,
I see it,
I am not blind.
They are behind.
As I meditate, I levitate.
Ascending,
Raising my frequency.
I am so high.
So high, the signs are right before my eyes.
In my mind,
Time travelling.
To the 4th dimension.
A parallel universe where there is two of us.
I'm just a star girl, star gazing.
Somewhere is a starboy praying, too...

God, life is so amazing.
It's unbelievable.
I feel like anything is achievable.
Like I've found the cheat code.
The secret formula.
I know the truth.
I saw it all with my own 3 eyes.
The universe is sending 4 me.
The morning call.
I am the chosen one.
Mother of the flock.
The golden fish.
The coolest kid on the block.
They call me weird for talking how I talk
but if you know what I'm saying
Then hey, you're a cool kid too.
Don't let the others fool you.
Travel with me.
Enlighten yourself.
Learn from the world.
We are one.
What a surprise,
to see ourselves in each other's eyes.
We're on a trip.
Watch everything spill like drip.
When they ask 'What does it feel like?'
That shit feels like paradise.

Sweet 16

Without a care in the world or a fuck to give.
Tonight, is the night we shall live our whole life
like tomorrow doesn't exist
and this can't be missed.
Because we are young
and it's the weekend
and I'm feeling good.
I'm feeling the vibes.
It's a lit night,
under these fluorescent lights.
So please don't stop the music,
Just dance.
Do it for the one time.
For the moments when we laugh and sing, cry and dream.
With our eyes wide open, not knowing...
If this is unforgettable or the night to forget it all...
But if it's one thing for sure,
We love it the most for the way that it made us *feel*.

Nostalgia

It's Saturday night.

Here I am writing about how I feel like I never left the party.

Like everyone went their own way once day came

and here I am with the music still playing,

dancing alone in an empty house.

I still hear my friends laughing

and singing along to the same songs

through the echoes of silence.

Like I've lost my sense of time

or maybe memories are timeless...

Last Love

Got me in my feelings.
Got me over here thinking...
About our last time, our last love.
Like do you wanna?
I really don't want it to be our last time.
Can we make it last, love?
Like do you wanna?
Do you wanna love like we used to?
I left the door open for you
in case you wanna come through.
Wanna replay me and you
cause I'm really in the mood.
So can you just spend one night with me?
Even if we ain't meant to be,
we can still live out our fantasies.
Cause you're the best I ever had.
Greatest of all time.
So will you be mine?
Just like old times...
Can we replay?
Like the good ol' days...
Cause when I'm with you, nothing else matters.
So can you be my last love?
Can we make it last, love?

Come Back

You will come back to me.
Someday, in some way...
As a dream,
as a bird,
as a song,
as a lesson,
As the smell of fun.
Like a distant memory,
I will recognize you time and time again.
Because I know your secret.
So I'll smile back so mischievously
because how could I ever forget your ways?
I'll catch you at every corner
because I know your every move.
You will come back to me and when you do...
I'll know it's you.
Hello again old friend, I remember you.

Something About Love

The funny thing about love is that it's never who, how, or when
you were expecting it to be like.
Maybe you pass love at the grocery store or at a party.
But you were too busy picking fruit or taking a shot of Tequila.
Maybe love is in NYC.
Maybe love is the girl you met on vacation in Mexico.
Maybe love speaks a foreign language.
Maybe love is in a different time zone.
Maybe love is still in love with another lover.
Maybe love is not ready for you.
Maybe you are not ready for love.
Maybe love isn't marriage.
Maybe love is to live for somebody, not to live with somebody.
Maybe love prefers coffee in the mornings
but that's not your cup of tea.
Maybe love binge watches Netflix series
but you prefer a book instead.
Maybe love is your mirrored opposite.
Maybe love is your same sex.
Maybe love is in a platonic relationship.
Maybe love doesn't know love.
Maybe the next time you meet love is 20 years after the breakup.
Maybe love is meant to only stay for 3 months.
Maybe love stays a while and builds a home.
Maybe love must go.
Love arrives exactly on time
and love leaves once it serves it's purpose.

How Deep Is Your Love?

What's your love like?
What's your Venus sign?
I want to learn how to love you if you're going to be mine.
I want a love that's soul deep up in my solar plexus
that it feels like Sunday morning breakfast.
Feels like climbing the highest mountain like Everest.
The deepest love to ever exist.
Something that'll make me say
'I never thought we could connect like this'
That's how deep this love is.

Rock Stars

Show starts at 9 so come on time.
We are going to put on the greatest performance.
This one is for the lovers.
and so the show began...
I fell in love with the boy in the band.
The rock star with the big black guitar.
Every night was a show and the stage was our home.
Living out our fantasies,
no celebrities, just lovers who happen to be rock stars.
We are so creative the way that we make love.
Head bangin'
We played our instruments...
Pulling all of our strings, so in tune,
moaning sweet melodies.
He said,
"baby, sing to me for you look pretty when you cry"
You're my rock and I'm your star.
Not even for the cameras this is truly who we are.

Intergalactic Love

Hey Adam, I could be your Eve girl.
I could create a whole world.
Plant your seed inside of me.
Can't you see inside of me,
my love for you to grow a family.
So give me all your kisses baby.
I feel the joy...
Of wanting to create a life.
I feel it deep inside.
It's like every time we make love,
we always seem to become one.
You are my sun,
so kiss my moon.
Bring me light,
a star is to bloom --
From our eclipse in this room.
So hey, let's make it happen.
Come inside,
make yourself at home.
We can watch the garden grow.

My Honeymoon

I held your face in my palms
like the crystal ball.
I swore I saw my life in your eyes.
like the starry night,
you can be my shining knight.
White horse and a carriage
Are you ready for marriage?
Because I want this for life.
The type of love I thought only existed in my dreams
came true with you.
Oh honeymoon,
You stay gold Mr. handsome boy,
You never fold soldier boy,
You're the man baby boy.
Let's go hand in hand.
Let's show the world our rings.
We made it so far,
a love so rich, we got an expensive thing.
So let's pop champagne.
It's a celebration of love.
I waited all my life.
The crystal ball was right...
Love at first sight.

???

Have you ever come to think...

You are the result

of a prayer that has been manifested some time ago?

Z3N

Remember to take a moment & just breathe...

Present

You're exactly where you need to be.

Dreams & Nightmares

11:11

I wish someone had told me

that not all love is destined the way you expect it.

I wish someone had told me

that not all things are meant to be understood,

but to be respected.

I wish someone had told me I'd get lost,

really lost. But that's a part of the journey.

I wish someone had told me

that sometimes the world will feel like it's ending...

but the sun will shine again.

I wish someone had told me that I'd be better than who I am.

So, I should be patient with myself because the grow up is real.

I wish someone had told me to chase my dreams

rather than trying to make sense of chemistry.

I wish someone told me they were proud of me on regular days.

I wish someone had told me life gets rough

but that's what makes you tough enough.

I wish someone had told me love won't always be reciprocated

in the same way but please, don't throw your love away.

I wish someone had told me that change is inevitable.

I wish someone had told me that I won't have it all figured out

but the attempt of wanting more will drive me...

Choose Your Move

Every move is made from love or fear.

Fear is what's going to hold you hostage.

Love is what keeps you going.

Promiscuous Girl

Fresh out the shower
and my hair smells like flowers.
I can't wait to put it down for you tonight.
Let's set the mood,
let's get it right.
Light the candles,
burn the incense.
Make me cum through my sixth sense.
Kiss my third eye.
My favorite kind of intimacy.
Beg for it like 'stop teasing me'.
So I'll ride for you,
ride on you and rock the boat.
I'll cause a scene, I'll put on a show.
Make us your favorite movie.
Our love is so cinematic...
We deserve a trophy.
Dive in my south pacific.
You say my flow feels holy,
Only, for you.

Nirvana

The nights we tripped acid,
I couldn't stop laughing so hard I cried.
It felt like only we existed.
When we loved,
I came to my senses.
Out of this world.
Paradise,
so heavenly haunting.
Feeling every emotion at once.
We saw the same thing and felt the same way.
All in one look and no words to say.
We poured our souls into one another.
I know how you feel.
I believe telepathy is real.
We've come to the realization that we have all the answers.
Key to life.
Keep this bond tight.
Don't tell our secret.
Promise to keep it.
Holding hands,
be my partner for life.
I swore we reached nirvana...
The nights we tripped acid.

Is This Everything?

I persuaded myself into thinking it doesn't get better than this.
You are the sweetest thing I've ever known--
Just like candy.
Do you know how addicting that can be?
How naive of me to think that I have tasted the purest form of sweet
and anything after us wouldn't add up
to the number of butterflies in my stomach
I get when I look at you. Heart eyes for you.
Not seeking no further than my eyelashes,
not daring to love beyond my love as is,
as if, we're the only lovers left alive.
You got me addicted to your love--
Just like candy.
I tell him 'put me on your tongue and taste me'.
He tells me I'm a sweetie.
We both on one.
I'm on him and he on me too.
Connected all 3.
Man, the shit that love will do.
Now we candy crushin'. Look at all this lovin'.
Or is it just the drugs talking?
Psychedelics got me going crazy.
Are you or are you not my baby?
Am I just your fun girl?
Or am I really your one girl?
Do you want this for life? Or is it just for one night?
So I wonder, does it ever get better than this?
Is this forever or does it end after the kiss?
What is this? Is this everything?

Devil Wears Prada

Murder is what she wrote.
As she kisses the paper she smokes,
then licks her sword because revenge is sweet.
Sexy savage got that look in her eyes.
Medusa when she looks at me.
She got me in her love spell.
This is a beautiful hell and she's a hell of a woman.
She knows what she's doing.
I swear, the Devil wears Prada.
and she came dressed to kill.
Not with horns and fangs and all those evil things.
It's the way she walks like she talks.
Pretty feisty if you ask me.
He asked nicely,
'Lady, could you be my bad thing?'

Tongue Of Daggers

Every time we spit at each other, it's always fire.
In the flame, I catch our burning passion.
Tongue of daggers hitting right where home is
and home is where the heart is.
& that's how I know,
our love is still alive...

A Hopeless Place For Love

I've been so caught up doing my own thing, I will admit that for you.
I don't have time, I can't commit mine to you.
It's just so hard trying to open up like I used to.
So many times I have drowned,
I don't want to be let down.
So, right now, this is a hopeless place for love.
I've had enough.
So go about your day.
I'm having it my way.
And you can't tell me I didn't say...
'I've been so caught up doing my own thing'.
I'm just trying to get right for me.
Would you still love me?
Even if you and I didn't work homie?
Would you still clap for me?
Or would you leave me out in the cold?
Would you fold on me?
I just hope you see my light from within.
This is not me moving on from you to him.
I just been so caught up in my own world.
I don't have time, I can't commit mine to you.
I can't give my love all for you.
You can't be another heart that I let down.
I told you from the go what it is.
Nothing too serious.
Right now, this is a hopeless place for love.

The Weekend

You are my greatest escape on the weekends.
Living a double life, I am no normal girl.
On the weekends, I feel like a rockstar.
I put on my night fit, do my hair real big.
Driving through the city with my clique.
Party next door, we get lit.
Then I tell my girls I'm leaving with you.
And we love and we laugh.
Then we dance and we crash.
Chasing the night away...
But you drove me to a place I cannot stay.
You made me feel good temporarily.
Pardon me, sometimes I forget my part.
That I have no place in your heart as anything more than.
I needed something more to believe in.
I needed more love to breathe in.
I needed something more than the weekend.

Lust Demons

I know they want me, but they could never love me.
Just fuck me but fuck them cause lust gets pretty ugly.
I know they want my energy --
but that's something they can't get from me.
I'm protected by the most high.
They can't bring me down.
These demons they're calling my soul.
But I say fuck all of you hoes.
Ain't no future, just one night.
Why do bad things feel so right?
I'm always tempted but I have to fight.
I can't let them win,
I can't let them have the chance to say that I let them in.
You know, I know
exactly what this is...damn lust demons...

Gemini

How dare you show a face that's not your own.
I guess we saw the real you but who would've known?
Two-faced like a Gemini.
You ain't have to lie,
or wear a mask to hide.
This is no masquerade party.
Come as you are.
There is no pleasing everybody.
Just love who you are.
We hear your cry for help.
But only you can save you from yourself.
Face your insecurities.
Find your purity.
Then you'll be sure to be...
At peace internally,
yourself truthfully.

Wicked Schemes

I see you had your wicked schemes.
Had a few tricks up your sleeve.
You did me grimy.
Played for the other team and stood right beside me.
Now, I see your true colors.
Are you trying to hide from yourself or others?
You're so fucking hard to believe.
Don't get mad when I catch on to your wicked schemes.
When I see it for what it is
and not for what you trying to deceive.
Shit like this gives me PTSD.
You really can't trust nobody.
Not even my homie that stands right beside me.
Isn't that crazy?
How you can't face me?
Say wassup if there's really a problem.
Friends turn to enemies,
so I drop them.

Batman

You're blind my love,

by love you're blind,

you're blind in love,

my love you blind.

Kryptonite

She knows he ain't no good for her.
You see the way he dims her light.
So, girl you should quit running back
like you lost your sense of self.
Like your superpowers don't work no more.
I'm tired of hearing you cry for help.
You know what to do.
Don't ignore the truth.
Don't keep running from your life.
Don't keep looking for warmth on a lonely night.
Looking for somebody
to spark your flame and hold you tight.
Hoping it'll last for life.
Thinking that it might be something worth the fight,
knowing it ain't right,
just right for the night.
Let the truth be told...
It's kryptonite.

Lost In Paradise

Truth is, there is no happily ever after just a once upon a time.

We're all so caught up in this fairytale where none of it is real.

Where everything is so perfect in that world.

We hear no evil, see no evil, speak no evil.

We believe that people are supposed to

live up to the characters we expect them to be.

When in reality, it's not like that.

Remind us of our gravity.

This is not Alice In Wonderland.

That's all in your head.

To be honest, this life is a series of unfortunate events.

I hate to break it to you kid,

But don't always believe that glamorized shit.

All that glitters isn't gold.

As you get old,

the truth unfolds.

You'll see this world is cold.

That's why we escape to fantasy.

Welcome to ecstasy.

Just don't get *lost in paradise.*

Insanity

How is it that you can feel so weak,
yet empowered at the same time?
Have you ever been heartbroken and in love all at once?

Oxymoron

Such an oxymoron.

To be a beautiful catastrophe.

To live for love like oxygen,

and to die for love by loyalty.

Just Like You

How you say you feel at home with me
when you have a whole family?
How you say you love me,
then talk crazy about me behind my back?
Like where did the love go?
Where's the trust at?
Did you forget about all that?
How do you dream of me and sleep next to her?
Am I just your ecstasy?
Your escape to fantasy?
Am I just your mistress in a black dress?
Am I being rebellious just like you because I like this too?
Am I?
I am the girl who knows the game, just like you.
I don't play by the rules, I bend and snap.
I'll throw it right back.
Like fire and fire,
You've found your match.
I'll do all that to tease you.
Then tell you that you can't have me the way that you want.
You can't have your cake and eat it too.
Don't I sound just like you?
Now how the fuck you think I feel?
I feel fly, just like you.
I make my own moves, just like you.
I got options too.
I'm bad, just like you, motherfucker.

The Light Of Your Life On A Dark Night

You told me I looked like I was in love but I was the only one.
I see it in your eyes,
the burden in you when you tried to smile for me.
I see it in your eyes, the emotion all out of you.
I see it in your eyes every time you were absent.
I could hardly recognize you,
I couldn't feel you,
I tried to heal you.
Night after night,
I came to you,
and I stayed for you.
I imagine this is what it feels like to dance in a graveyard
with skeletons who have no souls.
You lost all hope.
So, I vowed to help you love life.
Holding your chin high,
promising it'll be alright.
But I am nobody to heal you,
trying to fix you.
All I can do is be here for you.
Be the light of your life.

Deja Vu

Different place, same situation.

Why does life keep repeating itself in different locations?

I see the recurrence.

Perhaps, I haven't learned my lesson yet.

Figuring out what's best for me,

I decided to move differently.

Maybe then I can quit asking 'how come?'

Maybe then I'll get a different outcome.

Love Is Rage

We screamed and we cried because we gave a fuck.
And if we hadn't, we don't care enough.
When all is said and done,
the silence means the rage is over.
But as the show goes on,
and we lock eyes,
for the first time,
somewhere in the madness,
we find that Love Is Rage.

Queen Of Hearts

Got me sitting pretty high up on a pedestal.
And you're a man that sits high up on the horse he's on.
So high, come down.
See it for what it is now.
I never asked you to take me to the city,
drip me in Gucci and keep me pretty.
Because behind closed doors it's a different story.
I don't want to hold you by the heart when my feelings are not the same.
I don't want to stay here anymore.
You find ways to show me your love
but designer is not enough.
I can careless about the fancy things.
Stop living in a fantasy.
Can't get mad at me when I act out
of the character you thought I should be.
Quit, lying to yourself boy
You're all gassed up, don't let the high go to your head
That's why I spoke the crazy shit that I said
I wish we didn't abuse love like a drug.
Only see love as a soulmate instead.
But we had different views.
You didn't see this through, did you?
Now I want absolutely nothing to do with you.
How are you going to play the queen of hearts like a joker.
Ain't shit funny when you broke her, broken boy.
Now she's a temple you can't call home anymore.
You lost your privilege of fucking with a goddess.
So, all praise to your highness.
No thank you, I can put myself up on a pedestal.

Forever the queen of hearts no matter how you play her.

Sweet Ol' Venom

Sweet Ol' Venom like a Scorpio.
All those toxins need to let it go.
Just let it flow...
You're holding on to a past
that's making you view everyone as evil.
Resentment is bad for you.
I never did no bad to you.
Quit making comparisons from all the bad
that's been done upon you, before me.
Quit giving the aftermath
of the poison the people before has fed you.
I don't deserve that.
Give yourself a chance to fall in love with something new.
I could be so good for you.
Even when sweet ol' venom is all you're ever used to.

Wildcat

Where the fuck is your energy?
Nah, I don't feel you, you ain't hitting me.
But I should make you feel me good.
Don't forget I'm from the hood
You talking like you wanna get flipped.
Don't be surprised when you get whipped.
I'll show you my grip.
Cause I murder these bars
like ko, you'll see the stars,
might catch a charge.
I go so hard,
I should hit that bitch.
Make her throw a hissy fit.
Then I'll throw her kissy lips.
I should work that bitch,
turn around and twerk that shit.
Throw the same energy back, back, back.
I'll rock your shit, no rocket ship.
But I'll blast you bitch.
Don't talk that shit.
I'll spit on you just like this.
Yeah, you just got dissed.
I'm a wild cat.
So excuse me miss, you are dismissed.

Schizo

I need something to ease this pain,
this silent rage inside of me.
I need something to kill my demons
who scream at me so violently.
How do I cope?
Pop one, sip some, blow smoke.
Should I off myself or run with hope?
This ain't no joke.
I've been a victim of my own thoughts.
Trying to escape the same mind that traps me.
I'm not mentally ill, I'm intellectually skilled.
I cannot go against the will.
As a prophet, I must fulfill
the purpose at hand.
Stick to the plan
It's all a part of the story.
The horror won't last.
We'll have a good laugh.
When we make it to our glory.

Not So Pretty

I don't know why you still believe in me.

I'm not always so pretty.

Tell me what you see in me.

Is it the way that I show love?

Beyond my long hair and thick thighs,

painted lips and brown eyes.

That gets you mesmerized.

Cause I don't know why you still believe in me.

I'm not always so pretty.

Today I have no appetite, could you cancel dinner tonight?

I can't seem to bring myself to the table.

Up all night and I'm tired as fuck.

I don't want sex, I just want to sleep.

And I shouldn't have to explain.

I don't feel like talking.

At this point, just shut up and hold me.

Sorry for the breakdowns.

You didn't expect any of this trauma, did you?

I'm just way more complicated than you thought.

I can't promise I'll be good to you every day of the week.

I have my moments when I cry and I scream.

I'm not always the nicest, sometimes I'm mean.

I mean, I don't mean to be.

It's just sometimes this shit can get frustrating.
And instead of wearing my heart on my sleeve,
cause sometimes love can be hard to believe.
I let the wild cat in me off the leash.
Untamed, I let her hair loose.
I paint her nails pink.
So, you think I'm pretty, right?

Then claw at you and watch you bleed.
Which resembles the pain inside of me.
I told you, I'm not so pretty.
I don't mean to inflict my wounds upon you.
At least now we have matching scars like tattoos.
Engraved in your flesh.
And when anyone asks, you say my name till death.
Now do you still believe in me?
Once I've shown you how not so pretty I can really be?

Interviews

Painting the walls with my fingernails.
I tried to escape this room.
I came from a black hole,
hoping there'd be light at the end like I've been told.
You can get lost in darkness.
Sometimes the beginning is unknown.
So here you are in search of something
to reassure you that it's okay.
This is a sign, it's okay to not have all the answers.
Find yourself and once you do, your senses will guide you.
Listen to your intuition.
Knowledge is your torch.
Feel the fire inside, you are a lighthouse.
No need to feel like an orphan on the front porch,
lost and confused.
Be the one who knows about interviews.
When you take the time to learn about the inner you.

The Museum

As we walk through the valley of the shadow of death,
beware of the fallen leaves and autumn breeze
that reminds us to breathe.
Because what you're about to read, will be mind blowing.
You see, you need to trust yourself.
Walking into the unknown darkness
like you know your way around.
Can't let those demons bring you down.
Not when you got God on your side.
Keep on walking...
You'll come to find an abandoned home.
Who was once owned by a very small woman.
Who now likes to call this place 'The Museum'
She left a note on the kitchen table that reads...
"Welcome, please don't make yourself at home.
This is not a place to call your comfort zone.
This is a place for students to find themselves.
I left every door open because as soon as you walk in,
I promise you will want to walk out.
But the only way out is through.
Nothing to be afraid of darling,
This is actually the most historical place on earth.
Known for teaching people just like you
about the things nobody really wants to talk about.
So let's talk about it.

PS: Don't mind the skeletons in the closets,
they're cool. Sincerely, Olivia"

Door 1: Fear

Door 2: Insecurity

Door 3: Shame

Door 4: Regret

Visitors always questioned how she made her way
in a place so dark and windblown.
With only one candle lit that filled the room with of hope.
Olivia is a brave woman,
A wise one at that.
She had the courage to hang her skeletons in the closet
and call them ''cool' like
she knows how to make peace with her past.
She built the power to put her shame to rest
and realized this house is not a home to stay but a museum
for you and I to learn from then walk away.
And that's one thing Olivia didn't regret at all.
Because she knew her dark times would bring light
In due time ...
My name is Olivia and perhaps I am the living truth
That you can find your way out too.
And I hope this inspires you.
I still not stay in a place so clean and tidy,
but here I am, a woman who stands mighty.

Illusions

Sometimes you got to ask yourself...
'is it real or is it all in my head?'

Rebirth

Demolition leads to **evolution.**

Rhythm & Blues

Herstory

I lost my father,

then my brother,

but I am my sister's keeper,

And because of my mother,

I am the extended version of a teacher.

I found myself,

Lost.

Then learned to become the leader.

Mama's Interlude

I'm not saying I'm the perfect woman,
or that I have no flaws, and I do no wrong.
Because indeed I do.
Some days I'm a sad girl, a crazy lady, a mad woman, too.
I'm still learning this life as much as you.
I never said I had it all figured out --
But always remained true.
My love,
the love I made to give you life...
Beyond me and all for you.
You make me so proud.
Damn mama, you're the man mama.
Showing up as my mother and my father.
So many nights of silently screaming into my pillow
cause the rents been due and I got to feed my baby.
Shit has been out of hand lately.
The neighbors calling the cops
cause mama fighting with my pops.
That nigga going to leave me for a girl with no soulfrito?
I promise you my love will never compare
because her love will never come close or equal
the bond that we share.
What is this now that we see other people?
What happened to the family?

I thought it was us over everything.
Even when you go on...
To realize maybe things weren't meant to be,
I hope you still remember me.
Of where you came from and who taught you.
At weddings and family gatherings,
birthdays and funerals,
gardens and beaches,
courtrooms and somewhere in the bleachers,
forever rooting for you.

-Mama's Interlude

Her Side

Tell your mama, tell her the truth.
I bet she'll understand my pain
like your daddy put her through.
Funny cause you said
you never want to be anything like that dude.
But the sins of your father passed down to you.
Now here you go doing the same thing.
The same things I thought you'd learn from
to be better than that...
but I guess you learned to be just like that.
Boy, go wash your hands before you dare point a finger at me
like it's my fault for the baggage of your childhood trauma.
I don't need the drama of reliving the relationship I seen
my father have with my mama.
May we break the cycle and call this the beginning of the end.
Sometimes I wish I could go back in time
and thank the women who told me
how history will repeat itself
but only if you let it.
I would say it took a lot of paticncc to forgive
both you and myself.
I imagine that's what your mother had to do herself.
After trying to heal a broken boy, she lost her joy.
She had to undo herself.
Let go of the pain and the past.
All for a better health.

Girl, let him be a man of his own.
Let him see for himself.
That I wish I would have known.
But now I finally understand...
Your mother's pain as a woman.

-*Her Side*

Love Triangle

Mr. Fisherman

To her:

Did he compliment your wings and your fishtail too?

Did he like to swim in your ocean when it's blue?

How he got us Pisces hooked like fools.

Thinking we're the same man's one and only.

Girl, I know how your heart feels.

We should leave that man lonely.

He put a gun to our sun

and for all he has done, you can keep him if you please.

We both know it can't be me.

Enough to and fro,

you can be the one to drown in a sea of sorrow.

Woman to woman though,

I thought I should let you know,

It's time to let go.

Rock with your own flow.

A girl like me,

a fly ass Pisces.

To him:

Shame on you Mr. Fisherman

You wanna switch sides?

Bet, we can play a you like a middleman.

No tug of war or monkey in the middle,

It's up to you to solve this riddle.

How you love two women at the same time?

How you do two women so slime?

Doesn't that fuck with your mind?

Shame on you Mr. Fisherman.

You think you can just have the best of both worlds?

Because you can't decide on me or that girl.

Only for your selfish desires

you keep up with the same pathetic lies.

Don't you get tired?

Running game on women you promised lifelong.

Polygamy isn't my kind of song.

I don't do features.

So if you're having trouble deciding, don't side with me.

I see how you're moving, funny movement ain't okay with me.

I never wanted a superman

I just wanted a man to choose *me* over and over again.

Leave Me Lonely

I remember waking up next to you

in the morning, after a long night

of what I felt was intimate.

Only to question if you still love me the same.

Were the feelings mutual

or was I bad for living in that fantasy?

Bring me down to earth,

remind me of what it's worth.

I remember staying up late,

no rest at my kingdom,

all lonely,

drowning in my own tears hoping you'd save me

Save me like you said you would.

Save me like a savior should.

Save me like only I could...

Save me...

From the tsunami I've cried,

I built me a boat to sail or I will turn blue wading for you...

My Dear Valentine,

Thank you for the roses I had to die to receive.

With all my heart, fuck you.

In other words, I hate you.

However, I love you.

One by one, I picked the pedals off

Like, do you love me or love me not?

Let me remind you in case you forgot.

We've been through a lot.

I stood by your side my dear valentine.

I had your back like bonnie and Clyde.

Partner in crime, I know the bizz.

You know what it is.

You lit my fire, you had me faded.

All for your love.

Now look at us.

Remember what we discussed?

When things get real,

remember who kept it trill.

Remember the kill,

the honey that spilled.

Our love was a thrill,

our love was fatal.

Painful when we laid it out on the table.
You ain't play your cards right.
When you think I'll never go I just might.
I don't want to fight...

I'm already fucked up.
By shit I could have missed.
I should have missed you.
Instead I dressed up for you.
Dinner for two.
Water please.
For the roses I've been dying to receive.
The girl you left with no choice but to leave
because you didn't know how to hold a glass flower.
So you watched her shattered right before your eyes,
never to realize your own self
in the reflection of a million pieces...
I hope you enjoy the view.

Young Blood

This is all your fault.
I know I should have fought
A little harder against you.
Now you beat me black and blue
And I have to live with the thought because of you.
Now I can't open up to just anybody.
I know what it feels like to be used and abused.
When I was attacked,
nobody noticed.
I felt hopeless.
I mean, look man,
what if that was your mother, or your sister, or your daughter...
wouldn't you rather make her laugh than cry harder?
Your grip so strong, tight and heavy.
She was never ready...
You don't own me.
Stop trying to control me.
You're not for me.
Get off me.
Don't touch me.
The safe words you heard her scream
But can't you feel her pain?
Teary eyed, all bloody, nose runny,
dripping in the pouring rain.

How dare you?
Her flower is sacred.
Don't force shit.

If only you could have waited.
Now you got her feeling jaded.
Now she's afraid to love again.
She don't want those other men.
She don't want none of them.
The way Hennessy made you violent.
You turned me violet.
Beat me black and blue,
numb and misused.
How dare you?!

The Beauty In The Beast

The beauty in the way you've eaten me alive.

Then lied on my name.

Filling me with pleasure.

Then leaving me with pain.

Though, something about pain intrigues me.

Believe me to be a masochist.

I can't get enough of your tough love and sweet kiss.

Something about it makes me feel like I need this.

Sweet Ol' Venom, seducing me so fiercely.

Fearlessly, I don't beg for mercy.

I know we can switch roles; I can take control.

I can tame the wild beast in you with the beast in me.

When I aim to please,

I can make this a beautiful death.

But you rated r murdered us.

How could I mistaken love for lust.

So fatal, so brutal, so deadly, this is crucial.

So beastly the way you know the way.

Taken me out to the deep end then leave my love astray.

You got me fucked up, I am confused.

I feel misused by the way you just do what you do.

Beautiful yet beastly.

Killing me softly.

Is this love you say you have for me?

Eventually, you'll pay what you owe.

You'll reap what you sow.

Then It'll be clear to see ...

The ecstasy in agony,
The beauty In The Beast.

Numb

It hurt so much it didn't hurt anymore.

Or maybe I learned how to carry on

with scars that no longer bleed,

but remind me of where I came from.

As many times as I wanted to jump outside of my body

and leave this 3rd dimension behind me,

my bones became immune to the pain.

I've collapsed several times

before my skin grew tougher than wool.

My red kisses is really blood on my lips,

Blue inside like I bang with crips,

I'm just so numb to this shit.

Or maybe I learned how to carry on with scars

that no longer bleed but remind me of where I came from.

Maybe I really ain't numb.

I just feel things less these days

But less is more in a way...

More like so many emotions bottled up.

I just drink what's in my cup.

And you can try to numb the pain but It'll never go away...

Don't fill the void, face your fears.

Acknowledge the feels.
You too, can carry on with scars that no longer bleed
but remind you of where you came from.

Madly

We used to lay up at sundown.

When the day was through,

I needed you to hold me from the war going on outside.

You were my peace of mind until you pierced my mind.

Although this be madness, you are my sanity.

Romanticizing this bed of thorns,

in hope someday I see flowers born.

As I patiently waited for the sun, I danced with teardrops.

This love was so madly,

This love was like Shakespearean tragedy.

Love Sick

It's not easy to be with another

when I want no other.

I don't want to start all over again.

I don't want to waste time getting to know him.

When I know my heart doesn't belong to them.

Nobody does it like you do it.

Is this love or am I just used to it?

Is it time to let it all go?

Love myself just a little more?

After you, I learned to lock my doors.

I don't want to fall in love again...

That shit hit me to my core.

So let me go, let me go.

I need to find something to heal my soul

Cause baby, I'm lovesick.

The Coldest Winter

Days spent inside than out.

Warm and cozy,

cold and lonely.

If only you were here to hold me.

In this frosty snowfall.

The most wonderful time of the year

don't feel the same without you here.

I still remember the day my sister became a widow

and i lost my brother.

The kids lost their father

and I couldn't look at my mother.

So many xanax, I could tell she wanted to go with him.

I seen how she would gather her bones

and make dinner anyways.

She'd tell everyone to eat and just stared at her plate.

Every now and then I catch her staring off into space.

Every December 21st, my heart still breaks.

If only I can have one more day with my brother,

one more day with my father,

one more day with my lover...

Here I am dreaming by the fire,
burning like the coal.
Boots and a fur coat.

Last Christmas I gave you my heart.
Oh, what a time.
Now this is the coldest winter
cause you're not here by my side.
Everybody smiles but I hear their silent cries.
You should be here...
What my true love gave to me is the coldest winter of all.

Bad Romance

Did I not make it clear we were fading?

Did you forget how you had me waiting?

While you were out here chasing...

A dollar and a dream

And a bitch who's a fan for the team.

I'm a queen.

Did you forget how to come correct?

I gave you my everything.

I don't deserve disrespect.

So I'll go my own way, I'll do my own thing.

I keep it on my mind now.

"These guys will make time for want they want, anyhow.

They will do you dirty just to see how much you'd stay down"

But I'm up now.

So look at the flick of the wrist.

look at the girl you missed.

Chasing a one hit wonder.

You went wrong when you gave her your number.

Now you stuck looking stupid cause she aint even half of me.

So you can keep her and you can keep your distance.

Cause I want no parts of your half time love.

Left For Dead

Why did everyone dip out on me like that?
Why was I left alone to figure this shit out on my own?
I sat in the dark with my conscience out loud.
Silence is so loud.
I'm screaming my soul out.
I thought we were partners for life
Y'all left me for dead.
My blood is fresh, leaking up out of my flesh,
I'm wounded.
I have to revive my own self.
I can't lay bare on the pavement.
I can't sell myself short.
I fed you the only pieces I had left so that you can eat.
How nice of me.
I broke bread,
I shared my bed.
I'd hope you do the same for me.
But sometimes you be acting funny and it makes me question you.
And questioning my people
is something I shouldn't have to do.
Why you putting up an act?
That fake true shit ain't cool to me.
I'll fall back, I ain't with that.
Once you learn where you lack,
build your stack and secure where you're at,
Watch the electricity come back.

Did it all on my own.

Now I'm paid and full.

So don't come running back, trying to holla back

when you see me doing well.

Just know It's my turn to give you hell.

Sadderdaze

How is it that the clouds still hang above me?
I'm sick of sad days, stuck in a haze.
As I pray, I hope there will be better days.
Why haven't they come yet?
How long will it take?
How much will it take?
How much do I got to lose?
Don't you see I'm trying?
I'm tired too.
I don't have time to hit snooze
or else I'll lose.
Maybe I should work a little harder,
think more smarter.
But please, don't put a gun to me.
Patience is key.
I shouldn't feel like I have to run from me.
I just want to live life abundantly.
I've been waiting on you sunshine.
All I ask is to bring the sun to me.

Daddy's Little Girl

I ain't going to lie on you like you are a bad person.

But let's be honest,

you did some fucked up shit.

I heard what you said about me

in the kitchen the night you and mom split.

I knew you loved her and I but not enough to stay around.

I don't know my sister from that other woman,

but I hope she's doing well without you, too.

I remember waiting by the window for daddy to come home

only to get that phone call again...

"I won't make it tonight princess; I promise you next weekend"

Next weekend came around and it was the same line all over again.

Time went by and I grew into the young lady you never raised,

but taught not to fall for white lies and broken promises.

Not to wait around for no man to be ready.

By the look in mama's eyes, I could tell she was tired.

Not because of the inadequate amount of sleep,

but because she was fed up with your shit.

We were only trying to protect you but the streets wrecked you.

Where is home now?

Let Love Live

When you first laid eyes on me, you said I was a gem.
Like nothing you've ever encountered before.
That I am nothing like those other girls,
but how ironic of you to make me feel rivalry.
I knew I was the key to your core,
but my worries reside elsewhere.
Like to whom are you coming home to at night if not I?
Why is it my love that you deny?
Love is not supposed to hurt when I cry.
So, because of you, you ignite this goodbye.
But how could you?
How could you murder my sanity,
go against our vows and betray your own lips?
From the moment I questioned your love, I knew it was gone.
Thank you for being the epitome
of everything love is **not** supposed to feel like.
I know better now than to fall for an illusion.
I couldn't have you and keep myself too.
So, I've chosen me.
Loving you was a battlefield and I wanted to end war.
So, I made peace in solitude.
I'm finding balance in a world where we ask...
Why does life let love die?

Forever Ever?

Remember those times when we would stay up till sunrise?

Conversation always got so deep, our tongues would collide.

You always knew the right things to say.

You take my breath,

you have my word

and word is bond.

So I hold on trying to match your words with your actions.

No pillow talk, is you really about it?

I hope you are who you say you are.

I hope you aren't just leading me on.

Cause I love you just how you are.

I don't wanna find out

that you're really fucking somebody else.

Cause right here, right now feels so right.

When I look you in the eyes,

It feels like this could last for life.

So let's capture the moment.

Play your favorite song.

It feels like my birthday...

So I will have my cake and eat it too.

Watch me tremble at the taste of your love.

Remember I almost made you a family guy?

It felt so good I wasn't thinking about the future.

All I knew was I wanted you to be in it.

Every moment was intimate.

So tell me, is this forever ever?

I Told You So

I should've listened.
I knew but was too afraid to believe in the truth.
That there is no us.
I should've listened the first time you told me.
That we could never be.
That you could never be in love with me
or the man of my dreams,
and all that I hoped for.
And who am I to beg for love like a dollar
from a person with a hollowed heart?
I should've known better than to give my glass heart to a boy
still trying to hold the world with broken hands.
I knew he couldn't be my man.
I knew I deserved more.
I knew I shouldn't have denied myself.
I knew I should've listened
when shit just didn't sit right with me.
I knew I shouldn't have to be told twice that this ain't it.
I should've set you free long ago.
You ain't in alignment with me bro.
I got to hit the road.
I hate to say it but I told you so.

October's Very Own

I'll never know how to prepare for farewell.
Goodbyes and letting go aren't my forte.
I'm still trying to be okay with your absence
Although at first it may be incredibly hard to fathom
that the space needed for growth is uncomfortable,
never thought the distance between us
would feel so liberating.
"You'll be so great without me" you said.
And you were right.
However,
this is still the hardest thing I've ever had to deal with.
It's crazy how time travels.
One minute it's all love and the next you're left with nothing.
You should be here.
I miss you.
You were my go-to whenever I needed somebody to talk to.
You always knew how to make me laugh.
At times I blamed myself.
I hated me for leaving you.
I hated you for leaving me.
I thought love doesn't ever leave.
I thought I was the bad guy.
I thought how could I?
How could you?
Leave me like it's nothing.
Many times, it was me who walked out, I'll admit that.
But you drove me away.
You didn't secure me how I needed.
So I stopped being insecure about the love I expected.
Instead it drove me to love myself more.

I'm sure this is what you meant
by 'you'd be so great without me"
So I'm going to take some time away to make sure I'm okay.
I swear life is a paradox.
The same things you love are the same things you hate.
How you hate me for being like you?
asking for space in the same room.
Then while away, miles away it's 'I miss you, come back'
so enjoy the moment
because that's something you can't ever get back.
This is all we have.
The memories of our historical disaster.
A blessing in disguise.
Despite our ways, I still pray for you.
I love you, I always will.
Thank you for your time.

Distant Lover

Out of town...
The weather is beautiful here.
I wish you had taken this trip with me.
It took everything in me to run away from you...
but I knew I'd be saving the both of us.
It feels good to breathe fresh air again, out on my own.
Sometimes flowers are better off unpicked
and to be admired from afar.
I think about you often, I wonder how you are.
It's very different here than what I'm used to.
I realize you learn a lot when you're out of your comfort zone.
Losing everything that you've ever known.
I lost my mind in my room last night.
I thought about us and what could have been if I had stayed.
Apart of me feels like we're in limbo,
like there's unfinished business.
But I've been finding my own way.
My time here has grown on me.
I've shed old skin, leaving my past life behind me.
But I still find myself wanting to text you cause I miss you.
Wishing you were in my bed but you're in my head
so I'll leave it here instead.
I'm writing this letter to let you know,
that even a million miles away,
I still keep you very close to me.
Even when *home isn't with me.*

Widow

She thought why not spend her entire life with him.

I guess life had other plans for them.

So now she waits up in her kingdom.

For her love that only knows freedom.

Trying to balance the space between them.

Now she's all alone...

Wishing he would come home.

She only ever sees him in her dreams.

Now she believes that telepathy is as real as it seems.

She hopes you get the message.

And when she goes out and tries to explore,

remembering that she is free to soar,

It feels almost impossible to find what she's been looking for.

The man of her dreams.

Which does not appear to come true

because she only ever had that with you.

So her friends will all laugh and make fun.

They'll think she's crazy for chasing a wandering star.

For plucking the feathers off all the birds,

ensuring that you are the one that is hers.

So she breaks their hearts in search for her love in return.

I Remember

My best poems are still blue.

In the depths of all of them, I find you.

My muse, everywhere I go.

In my mind, you're right there by my side.

I can hear your laugh,

I still see the way you look at me.

The girl of your dreams.

Remember you told me that?

You told me that you love my art

And every time I leave, you fall apart.

Because you see my passion and you love my heart.

Do you remember?

The way I sung to you

and kissed you too?

With the same lips that vowed I do,

cause I do.

Do you remember when you missed me?

Do you still do?

Remember needing to speak to me because I spoke the truth.

You loved my light.

Your golden girl.

I showed you freedom from this whole world.

Need I remind you of who I am?

Don't you recognize?

Don't you see your name written in between the lines?

Don't you remember all that you said to me?

Remember you said...

If reincarnation is real, you would recognize my soul again?

Don't you remember it got that deep?

I remember everything...

Daddy's Interlude

Hey you, I just want to say I'm sorry
for the way things turned out.
It was never meant to be this way.
My apologies for the times I ain't show up.
I know your momma be trippin'
but that's her way of showing love.
Your mother and I had our differences,
but we found a way to correspond.
I hope it isn't too late to respond.
I hope you forgive me for wasted times.
I hope you forgive me for my selfishness.
Even though it's too late to fix this,
I just hope you find forgiveness.
Everything that happens is meant for us.
When I was in the institution,
I didn't mean to cause you any confusion.
I hope you learned to differentiate a boy and a real nigga.
I hope you feel me when you listen to Pac, Nas and Jigga.
Don't be out here falling for these sweet-talking dudes
like poppa do.
My baby girl, you're my world.
Any guy who steps out of line, I'll pop him too.
Girl, you know what it do when it comes to you.
I just want to see you be successful and I just want to say
I'm so proud of you.

Never Again

I want to get apologized to for all that happened...

Cause we been through some shit

and I'm still trying to get over it.

Trying to forget all of the memories,

all of the damage done to me.

I got to forgive my past to find my peace.

I don't want you back, I got to leave.

So I'm going somewhere to make a better life.

So let go of me,

let go of you.

It came to a point when I knew

I can't keep spending all of my days on the eastside,

forgetting who I am on the other side.

On the inside told me there's more treasure to find.

So I got to get going...

I learned a lot about being here with you

and everything we went through.

Now I know I'm going somewhere to make a better life.

But sometimes I think, why couldn't we stay and make it right?

Fuck it, I got to get going...

So let's live our lives and support each other in whatever we decide.

Because who are we to desire a love we don't know how to give?

I must admit, the love we give can be scary if we become selfless
or want our love all to ourselves then we become too selfish...

Once upon a time, I lost myself loving you.
Now I look in the mirror and say
'You are the one I should be giving my love to'
 Love is the day you look your fears in the face and say
'nothing can stop me, not even you'

I Can't Stay

I can't stay to stroke your ego.

I can't stay to sacrifice my happiness for the lack of your own.

I can't stay to arch my back, half broken for your pleasure.

I can't stay to lose myself to keep you company.

I can't stay to fall for a lying king.

How dare you lie to me.

I can't stay to play cards with a cheater

when I'm the queen of hearts and you're the joker.

I can't stay to pay you attention like I owe you something,

I owe you nothing.

I can't stay to hear the reaper

call my name in the most exquisite way.

I can't stay to dance to deaths song which sounds so lovely.

I can't stay.

Remember how you left me?

Ballerina

When you think about my love for you,
you think I'd stay exactly where you left me.
Letting the sky fall down upon me.
But sugar, I'm going to get so fly.
My strength has taken me to a place where there is more to see.
Now that I am so far gone,
you'll never be able to get close to me.
Oh na na, you can't hurt me again.
The girl you once had in your palms now holds all the cards.
See how the tables have turned,
I've lived and I've learned.
I don't dance for you anymore.
For the world is my stage and I am her ballerina.
The show must go on without you...
So let bygones be bygones
and watch how I move on.

Don't Cry For Me

Please don't cry for me.

I hate to be a burden or the reason for your misery.

I don't need the sympathy.

I feel your empathy, it's like we're sharing this energy.

But my feelings are my own.

So let me cry alone.

Behind closed doors,

I cry alone.

On my bedroom floor I cry along to my favorite songs.

Cause I been to strong for too long...

In my bathtub I let my tears flow,

I let my fears go,

screaming lyrics from Keyshia Cole.

Like 'Let it go' Missy.

Trying to balance the highs and the lows.

I watched you watch me drown in sorrow,

then I knew I had to make a better day out of tomorrow.

I pick myself back up.

I had to rise above.

But when I'm low, I just want you to know,

Please, don't cry for me.

Silent Game

Silence was always one of my favorite songs we shared.

Sometimes fulfilling,

sometimes empty,

sometimes I don't know how you're feeling,

sometimes I understand completely.

In the absence of words,

I wonder your thoughts.

I wonder what you think of me.

I wonder a lot.

I wonder if it's only me.

I wonder if there's more than this, this silent game.

I wonder if you'll ever tell me...

Tell me what this means to you.

I really want to understand where you're coming from.

Sometimes it was I who held my tongue.

But that silence was so loud

and if you would have listened more,

you would have understood where I was coming from.

I promise it wasn't quietness to think nothing of.

I could feel it in the air when you breath...

You try to act like it's just me but I am not alone.

We both know...

Homecoming

I've cried horrendously for hours upon hours.

I sang sad songs on my windowpane

praying for the pain to go away

and never come back another day.

Life broke my heart to create this art.

Blood, sweat and tears.

I've faced a lot of fears just to make it here.

I've been sad as fuck.

Afraid to show some love.

Cause I've been let down too many times before

so I can't get my hopes up.

I don't want to catch myself crying on the bathroom floor

like what's love?

Can you remind me?

Cause this is not it.

I got to find a peace of mine.

I got to stop fighting my mind.

I should listen to myself.

Fuck that crying for help.

I got to reach the higher me...

So everything will be clear to see.

Fuck your conditional love.

What was I thinking of?

I should've came home to myself.

But now that I know my truths,

I ain't going back to you.

I've been down this road before.

I know what it leads me to.

I know better now.

As much as it hurts me to walk away,

It hurts me more stay.

And baby I can't die for you.

I gotta live for love.

Miss Me

Don't hit my line.

You fucked up the first time.

The first time I gave you my love,

you gave my love away.

Shame on you for fucking all this up.

I haven't spoken to you in months.

Don't tell me that you miss me

when you used to dismiss me.

Now it's fuck you.

You played me,

you played me, now you all played out.

Playboy, you played yourself.

Don't tell me that you saw this coming.

I don't care, don't tell me nothing.

I don't wanna talk.

I don't wanna listen.

Don't call my phone.

I'm good on my own.

Don't love me now because it's too late.

You missed me.

Cry Baby

Cry if you need to, tears are cleansing.

Release.

You

Today, I thought about killing you.

I thought maybe you'd be better off without me.

I thought maybe if I ended things here,
I would just be the girl you used to know.
Today, I thought about killing my ego.
I thought maybe there's a few things that I should let go.
Because no, I can't stay here anymore.
Fucked up too many times before.
How do I forgive someone who took my life to live?
I fed your ego, you killed my soul.
You can't blame me now that my heart is cold.
I just wanted you to show me love.
But now I point the gun.
Fuck you for what you've done.
I'm ready to go in for the kill
cause you never gave a fuck about how I feel.
Don't hit me with none of that 'how bout now?'
when you see me later.
Cause I'm so over it.
I thought maybe I should go
somewhere out of my body,
where no one can find me.
Look at what you've done to me.
Got me looking so crazy right now.
Got me ready to sing Man Down.
Got me looking so crazy.
I'm ready to end it all now...
Because of you!

The Switch Up

Oh my world, you have evolved on me.
I'm trying to keep up, but you keep on shifting.
People who promised they'd never switch up are drifting.
Who's really with me?
Nothing is the same,
things changed.
Seems like you don't want this love no more.
Like you got more life to explore.
Like I wasn't meant to be yours.
So please, don't hit me up when you're bored.
I don't got time for distractions.
I don't got time for fake love.
No, I don't even wanna makeup
I don't wanna pretend
like it's all good like I ain't ever lost trust.
But trust me I forgive however we lost us.

Now, I'm past all that.
I let time pass to heal that.
Still got love for you, no doubt.
But you did me wrong, now you crossed out.
Should've never did that.
Should've never let it get bad.
Now you better get back.
Cause things ain't the same.
You out here switching lanes,
fucking with them lames.
I won't say no names.
You know what I'm talking about.
Don't act clueless when I call you out.
I know I talk really loud,
touch you where it hurts.
Don't try and play me
like I won't bite back and make it burn.

Like I won't cause a scene in this bitch
and make you pay your homage.
Don't forget I'm a savage.
I could turn shit up but maybe I should chill.
I know that ain't my deal
to feel some type of way about how you never kept it trill.
Can't expect someone to keep it real with everyone else
when they never stayed true to themselves.
You played yourself trying to run game on me.
Now you mad at me?

Her Blues

Maybe someday I'll understand...
My mother's cries,
her sad eyes,
hurting inside.
She don't want to tell the kids daddy was a foolish man.
Never came home till 4am.
I always wondered where he gone again...
Why he never picked up the phone when I'm calling him.
How you treat your woman like this?
Perfect example
of the type of man your daughter should miss.
But she never thought she'd end up
with somebody just like you.
Who treats her just like this.
He makes her blue,
then gives her a kiss.
Somebody new but It makes her reminisce...
On the past I been through
when I seen my mother and her blues...

She told me to run as fast as I can
if I ever come across somebody like you again.
She told me to be smart this time.
Don't fall for the sweet lies,
don't let him cross the line.
Know when to draw the line.
I didn't understand until it was me this time.
It was me who was crying...
Sad eyes, hurt inside.
Who would have known I'd be just like you.
Now, I finally understand.
Her blues.

Thrill Of A Riot

I never thought I'd do it...
Never thought I'd ruin him.
Guess I was so broken, too.
My trauma causing drama.
Spilling all over you.
Falling to fast is something I knew we shouldn't do.
It'll be worth the wait, I told you.
But you wanted my love on demand
And I needed patience.
What don't you understand?
I wasn't ready.
I couldn't love you how you needed.
You didn't care.
You were selfish.
You had your demons.
I guess that's what made us so attracted...
we were broken.
Hoping maybe this time would be different.
But it isn't.
So we lost it...
To the thrill of a riot...

The Culture

14U2

I write for people like you
because I recognize a piece of me.
I know what it's like to be silenced
and screaming at the same time.
To run and not know which direction...
To chase winds and sail seas,
Just to go with the flow...
Now I create waves
for an audience who was just as lost as I was.

Fall Into Winter & Spring Into Summer

As we Fall into Winter,

the season of the soul,

the year comes to a conclusion.

The hours of darkness become longer

and we sit in classrooms and studios,

working inside to draw our resolutions.

Coming up with solutions

to make the future better than the past.

Both nostalgic and celebrational.

As we Spring into Summer,

the season of external exploration,

we become more physically awakened.

Ready for adventure.

The days are brighter, and the night life is wilder.

Playing outside in the warmth of fresh air.

Enjoying our sun kissed skin and not the wind in our hair.

Both memorable and celebrational.

Party like it's the early 2000's

Welcome to the party!
90's babies in the house.
Show them how we get down.
Music blasting hip-hop and R&B,
sounds like poetry.
Aventura, bachatame with me.
Bruking It down and dutty wining.
To Everyone Falls In Love.
So take my hand and together we,
will celebrate a life of dreams.
Grown folks all doing their thing.
As the kids wander, they laugh and sing.
Chasing fireflies and ice cream trucks,
playing man hunt and double dutch.
In your favorite red chucks,
getting scuffed up.
You better get dressed up,
you're growing up!
Get ready for the party.
Cheers to the weekend.
Cheers to the times we never thought would end.

United

You and I.

I am you.

We are one.

2 Of Cups

11/2

Individuality & Partnership

We do not belong to nobody.
We are not possessions.
We must find ourselves first.
We have our own journey.
We can hold hands,
we can be partners,
we can be ourselves with each other,
we can travel together,
we can share this life.
But for whatever reason the universe decides we shall part ways,
whether it be because we have served our purposes,
whether it be because we aren't meant to be
the piece to fit each other's hearts,
whether it be to see you later or death do us apart.
No love lost.
I wish you the best from however far and timeless.

This is a reminder to love yourself enough for the both of us ...

Sometimes we become
completely infatuated with our significant other.
Head over heels obsessed and attached
that we find ourselves in codependent relationships.
We find ourselves more in love with the idea of love
or the character whom this person plays in our fantasies,
rather than who they really are.
We rely on them for our happiness and we shouldn't
because happiness is something you go out there
and you achieve on your own.
Then you come together and share that joy with your partner.
We should love without attachment.
Love without expectations.
We should love unconditionally.
You're setting yourself up for disappointment,
as soon as the other doesn't live up to your expectations
or the potential you saw in them.
Suddenly, their wrong and we don't love them anymore
because they're not who we thought they should have been.
They aren't who we want them to be
and it crushes our idea/fantasy.
Truth is, we are wrong for this.
We need to learn to set our intentions
before entering a relationship.
Understanding what we bring to the table
and how far are we willing to compromise.
We need to learn to discover ourselves first.
Then connect and say
"this is who I am and what I know I want and deserve out of love"
Unconditional love is the ability to love someone
without pride, without a clock, without touch,
without expectation, without fear, without ego.
So when you love, make sure it's unconditional.
Make sure you remember your own individuality in a partnership.

Love

Love is to be free, love is not to be cuffed.

Brown Girl

I am not my skin, I am not my hair.
I'm just a woman who wants to be treated fair.
So, don't judge me on my brown skin
get to know me on who I am within.
I am a woman like her and her
and as a woman,
I was made to know the blood I came from.
I was made to know women are much more than their bodies.
Women embody the type of strength men could never carry.
So girl, let your hair down.
Don't be ashamed if your skin is brown.
Walk around like you run this town.
If they have something negative to say,
you shut them down.
I tell people all the time...
I am not my skin, I am not my hair.
I'm just a woman who wants to be treated fair.
Compliment me on my invisible things.
Like my gold soul or my character inside.
I shouldn't have to hide from those guys
who view me as candy to their eyes.
Like, can you not?
Can you not want me for my hair
or my brown skin cause that's not fair.
Look me in my brown eyes and see
that I am much more than that.

Would you love me still if I took off my makeup
and threw on my night wrap?
Or did I get a little too raw for you?
Should I have not taken it off for you?
Cause if you can't handle me in my element,
Then you don't deserve me in elegance.

High School

I remember in high school I was always either loved

or most hated and nothing in between.

The one who either stayed to herself or caused a scene.

I remember in high school,

we skipped school to get food and go on adventures.

Acting like hoodlums and hooligans.

I remember in high school, we'd skip class just to text.

Skipping class to deal with overwhelming stress.

Came to school best dressed or in sweats.

At that time, I was the most depressed.

Cried in bathroom stalls and smiled through the halls.

By noon, we had rap battles at the lunch tables.

I remember in high school,

I wanted to participate in the open mic event.

Every year I'd sign myself up

only to turn down the opportunity because I was too afraid.

Afraid that if I stood up on that stage, my anxiety would rage.

I should have faced my fears anyways.

I have a lot of shit to say.

But I guess saving it for later was a better idea.

Look at me now ...

I remember in high school, I couldn't promise nobody all A's

I remember in high school, I loved art class.

My teacher always encouraged me to pick up my pen more.

For that, I am so thankful.

I remember in high school, I loved science class so much.

I experimented with the law of attraction

and realized we are the creators of our universe.

I remember in high school, we always came to school high.

It was the only way we'd make it through the day.

I remember in high school, we couldn't wait until Friday's

just to party all weekend but let's not talk about it Monday.

I remember in high school,

we couldn't wait for the day it'd be all over...

Now it's all over and all we have left is

 "I remember in high school..."

Make A Wish

Remember wishing upon the stars and trying to believe!

Remember your birthday?

When you made a wish you promised to keep?

Well be careful what you wish for

because it never comes as you think.

But believe me it'll come...

Just never as it seems.

Stay High

The practice of mindfulness is the key to understanding life.

Awareness brings you to a state of higher consciousness.

Being observant will make you the highest person in the room.

I'm Trying

Trying to tell myself things happen the way they do
for a greater purpose even beyond my understanding.
Trying to convince myself that this is a blessing in disguise.
Trying to be more receiving of love in ways I don't recognize.
Trying to work on acceptance
even when I was the one rejected.
Trying to go on like I'm unaffected.
Trying to make peace with what it was and what it is.
Trying to respect the differences.
Trying to get it all on my own.
Trying to make my efforts show.
Trying to be somebody in life
even if that means I got to leave somebody to get right.
Trying to hold on and let go at the same time.
Trying to play for keeps and let go of what isn't mine.
Trying to keep a smile even if I'm not fine.
Trying to keep my balance and not step out of line.
Trying to understand your point of view.
Trying to see how things would be like if I were in your shoes.
Trying to leave and start new.
Trying to see a life without you.
Trying to find ways to make it through.
Trying to keep my sanity.
Trying to prevent myself from going crazy.
I'm trying...

Prayer: A Message To God

I pray I become better at being.

I pray for my self-control.

I pray I become the girl of my dreams.

I pray God keeps sending me signs to guide me in the right direction

I pray what's for me will find it's way.

I pray for the process.

I pray for the patience I need to get to where I want to be.

I pray for better days and not the same old routine.

I pray to keep the family close and always have food to eat.

I pray for my sister's peace.

I pray the men I love become the best they can be

with or without me.

I pray you remember the vows we made, unconditionally.

I pray these prayers come true.

I pray in the end I'm so proud.

I pray for my love.

I pray for the journey...

I pray, amen.

Balance

Perhaps this life wasn't meant to be lived happily,
but rather to be in a state of equilibrium.

Parties On The Eastside

The city that never sleeps.

Up till sunrise creeps.

We get it poppin' no chill.

What a thrill.

City hues and streetlights,

Moonshine, late nights,

pretty girls, cat fights.

High heels and kicks,

movies and skits,

pictures getting lit.

Fire up the ganja.

Bad gals and rude boys.

Tell the DJ play Painkillers

Tonight, we let ecstasy heal us.

So grab somebody and just ride it.

Baby, let's not fight it.

Smells like that teenage spirit.

Playboy perfume, shots in the bathroom,

lipstick stains and gold chains.

Doing things we aren't supposed to.

We head downtown for the show.

Rebellious acts of x and o...

Fuck what anyone has to say.
Our teenage runaway,
young and brave.
Our song, record on replay.
Dance with me, my love.

X

First things first, RIP X.

Mark my territory like X.

Out the trap, now I'm famous like Dex.

Fuck my ex.

Hardcore like triple X.

I remember the day we met.

I liked your style, I like how you dress.

I was so impressed.

Now I know you seen my text.

Remember what I said?

I want to travel to all 50 and touch a milly

and only my day ones are coming with me.

Pull up to the 610.

They wish they knew me back then.

Way back when I was a normal girl.

I told them I'll be great.

Manifested my dreams

now I'm eating a full plate.

I'm coming no matter how long it takes.

I'll arrive on my own time, call me fashionably late.

Traveling in and out of state.

Where are you from?

Rep your place.

Shoutout to the A.

Love from the east to the bay.

Shoutout to Los Angeles we lost angels in this.

ATL it gets hard as hell

and yeah, we tripped but we never fell.

Just a traveler with a story to tell.

So I saved it for the books.

I swear this shit isn't as fun as it looks.

I told ol' boy from Texas

I could never be his miss.

Told him put an X on his wish list.

This ain't none of his business.

Focus on yourself.

Plant a tree and give back to the community,

Donate to charity.

I'm just trying to save my people, pray for Puerto Rico.

I'm just out here trying to make a living.

Trying to leave a mark like X.

Fearless

No fear in my heart for a woman who bleeds like me.

No fear in my heart for a man who needs me.

Pray For Love

How is it that administration enforces education,

yet people still lack eye opening interpretations?

Y'all not woke following the rules and regulations.

Do y'all know see the everyday incarcerations?

Tearing families apart and causing separations.

Let's not raise another fucked up generation.

Let's be an inspiration, not a pathetic demonstration.

This is history in the making.

We the people,

let's do better.

Quit the procrastination.

Who gives a fuck about who this and who that.

Who's the realest and who's quick to stab you in the back.

Who's white and who black.

They keep on taking my people.

We just want to be equal.

Ain't no safety on my block,

ain't no peace outside my window.

There's way too much poverty.

This life keeps on pocketing me.

How much do you want from me?

How much weight must I push?

In the hood, I promise this ain't what you want homie...

The system of control is advancing technology to ruin humanity.

The media is the matrix, an alternate reality.

By invasion of privacy and operating robotically,

corruption leading to catastrophe.

I pray to god to protect my family.

This is my Ghandi.

Let's start a movement for improvement.

Let's pray for love.

Child's Play

We exist to reproduce.

To carry our species

so that we don't expire.

Youth is the season for which love is it's genesis.

So careful thought should be in child's play,

knowing that the years of life will reflect from it's birthplace.

Because the colors will show,

the kids will sing about it.

The show we play,

the kids will know about it.

The colors will drip,

the kids will cry about it.

But the kids will be kids even when they grow out of it.

Now we're still those kids.

This is me singing about it.

I figured it out,

how the colors play now.

How the show plays out...

I'm not afraid to admit that I cry about it now.

Motherly

Happy Mother's Day

to all the women who not only have children,

but have played the part.

Who have made sacrifices with themselves, by themselves.

For being the epitome of life itself.

All praise to this motherland.

Mother, thank you for the food you provide,

you've allowed me to grow.

Mother, thank you for being the best teacher,

I've learned so much.

Mother, thank you for your tender loving,

you know how to take care.

Mother, thank you for working overtime, you've got patience.

I know not every day there's sunshine,

but every day I pray we've got a little more time.

Every time mother, you came through for me.

I swear there's not one thing you wouldn't do for me.

So my apologies as a rebellious child,

If I ever made you question who your little girl is...

For all the back talking,

late nights I held you up,

phone ringing, sorry I ain't pick up.

For all the times I've gotten so caught up,

I didn't know how to show love.

My apologies.

Honestly, I couldn't thank you enough.

The way Quise and I grew up,

that's my brother.

Raised right by our grandmother.

Lady, what would I do without you?

Everything I do is for you.

Madonna

You are the closest person to God I know.

You are a beautiful soul.

I try to act like you're immortal.

But deep inside, I know one day they will call for you.

I know you're near the last level...

So thank you for your years of labor.

Thankyou, for your years of raising 11 broken children,

one failed marriage,

and a man who couldn't keep his promises.

Thankyou, for building this empire.

Dedication is in my DNA.

Dead or alive, I'll keep it in your name.

I'll be the daughter that keeps you young.

I see the way you watch me dance

when your bones are to fragile to.

Mama, have a seat.

Let me rub your feet,

make you some tea

You deserve the love you give.

Sisterhood

I am a girl like her and her and her.
Even if we didn't grow up under the same roof,
the same rules still apply, it's girl code.
As I help my mother with the garden, I realize...
Sister, we are the legacy of a woman
who knows how to do the groundwork.
We come from the same roots that keep us bonded.
And who's to say
we can't get a little down and dirty sometimes?
But never get too weak in the knees,
to fall for a man who can't bow down to us.
Don't give your pretty pink flower to these guys
who never gave you roses.
Girl, don't you forget your power, you better own it.
Don't let your tiara slip.
Paint your nails, gloss your lips.
Smile, show the world your pearls.
Don't forget your diamonds.
Spray your favorite fragrance.
They love the smell of a woman.
Lace up your corset tight enough you must sit up,
like the lady you are.
And if the lady you are decides to free the nip, then so be it.
Sister, shave your head if you please.
Rock the baggie jeans.

I am a girl like her and her and her...

Not falling accustomed to the image
of what a woman should look like.
Because the first woman I met had her hair tied, no makeup,
all sweaty from birthing a moonchild.
Spending most of her days under the sun,
watering the garden.
Giving no fucks about the dirt on her hands
as long as the kids were fed.
Generation after generation,
Sister, come as you are.
I know your blood.
I know what it is to be a woman.

Queen City

By my observations on the world we are,

from the workforce, to the household.

Women are told to be petite, submissive, and weak.

The grand source of our misery.

Perhaps, you've got the wrong idea on my fellow ladies.

Baby, don't forget where you came from.

A woman who knows how to stand her ground

shall not be held down or be held hostage,

like a disease of the mind,

or held accountable to secure his own insecurities,

or the lack thereof.

Women can be alluring mistresses, wives, mothers,

yet most of all, human too.

I've seen women intoxicated by the affection of men,

under the influences, pay them no true love.

The woman who has been taught to only please,

will soon find that her charms won't always woo

the men who overlook her love.

She will then focus her native energy into herself

for more love.

Whether she be loved or neglected,

her priority should be to

attain respect and morality for herself.

To practice self-worship

than to be intrigued by conditional lovers.

Not to fall for men who lie to her feelings

and forbids dancing with soul.

Which destroys her innocence and dark truth be told...

Men will draw conclusions which she little thinks of

but I hope she goes on

allowing intuition to guide her every move.

Because she will not model to suit his delicacies,

nor his idea of her.

Hey Baby

Hey baby,
I have a lot of work to do
but I promise, I'll be coming back home to you.
Let this woman handle her business.
Let's save it for the perfect time.
I've been waiting all my life
all for a love like this.
So I just want to let you know,
I want to watch you grow,
love you unconditional.
Oh baby, there's a special place in my heart for you.
I do this all for you.
I just want to make you so proud.
Tell the world your momma loves you so loud.
I even wrote this song for you.
Way before I even knew about you,
I just knew I had this love for you.
Cause you keep me grounded,
you keep me focused,
you keep me going,
It's so amazing.
Look what love can do.
I can't wait to meet you.

Winners Lose First

The universe speaks to you in code.

It's up to you to read in between the lines and seek the signs.

But sometimes I can't seem to find what I'm looking for.

Sometimes I don't know where I'm headed

or where this thing called "life" will take me...

All I know is I got to keep going.

I got to keep growing

I have to trust the process

and let go of things that don't help me progress.

Like fuck going out every weekend.

I need time to reflect.

I don't need the mess that comes with all of that.

I don't need to be spending all my cash.

So let me save this time.

'Everything will turn out fine' I repeat in my mind.

Maybe I had to lose first.

Maybe it's how this game is played.

And I know it doesn't make sense.

But everything takes time so I'm trying to have patience.

I'm trying to stay focused.

Keeping my eyes on the prize,

keeping my head in the game.

Winners lose first but I am not a sore loser.

So I'm back at it again.

I'm just trying to do the impossible

because I know anything is possible.

So watch me crush their doubt.

Show them what I'm really about.

All the setbacks and minor mishaps.

In the end, we'll look back like 'that was all so worth it'

I knew it would turn out to be perfect.

GCODE

You taught me everything I know

about the game and how to play.

You told me this was a different kind of sport.

Ain't no rules to this life darling.

But always remember to follow the g code

and some things only we know.

And make sure the people around you stick to the script.

Anybody will try to knock your hustle

when they see you doing good.

Just invest, flip and don't say shit.

Careful not to spill the beans.

Business is like chess.

Hold your cards close to your chest.

Make movements in silence.

I bet I moved you inside with this.

God is my only witness.

I tried not to get caught.

I brainstormed with my thoughts.

I cried as much as I fought.

But to the world,

I showed my crooked smile in between my dimples.

You always said I'd make a good actress

because I have the best poker face.

Even when my mind is racing, I still stay in place.

Home run, no second base.

Remember the GCODE, just in case.

Control

Land of the free but the system wants control of me.
Toxins even in the food we eat.
That's why I stick to the greens.
Herbs really saved my life.
It's fight or flight.
They want to get you one way or another.
If it ain't me then they're accusing my brother.
Young black man you better hold it together.
Don't fold under pressure.
I lost too many of my niggas
that made me who I am today.
Sometimes I don't even know what to say.
All I could do is pray.
Cause the pain is that deep, it scared me.
I could never take it away.
So I'm going to make it my way.
Nobody telling me what to be,
nobody controlling what I see.
Don't you mock me for what I believe.
You ain't chief.
Fuck the police.
Who's really protecting we?
I'm my only supreme.
Don't tell me when to leave.
Ain't this land of the free?
Who's really cuffing me?

Vice City

Wickedness lies in the dolla dolla bill y'all.

Fuck tax, bitch better have my money.

I've seen what people do when they're hungry.

I watched the closest to me, switch up on me.

Talk about loyalty but you were nowhere to be found.

You ain't really about the set you claim,

cause when I was down, you was out.

Man, what a shame.

Who would have thought you'd be the one to blame.

You think you know the game

but with what's next,

you might need a bulletproof vest.

I won't put my hands on you,

but don't think you're untouchable.

And that chick you're with could never be a Clair Huxtable.

She belongs to the city.

610 ain't always so pretty.

The neighborhood is really real.

The bros is in the field.

Yelling free them, free them.

All we want is freedom, freedom.

I lost sleep trying to figure my way out.

Trying to make it to the other side where the grass is greener

and the work is timeless.

But the greener the grass the more people are envious.

You just got to mind the business that pays you.

No label, stay true to yourself

before the industry claims you.

Because can't nobody love you like you do.

They just wanna eat off your dreams

because C.R.E.A.M.

Trapped

Do you know how many hearts were broken in courtrooms?

How many prayers were said

in hopes to have my boy come home soon?

How many jail visits I've suffered through

because even then, there's a wall between us.

But still we hold our hands up to the glass

like we praise each other from the inside out.

District attorney's trying to convince me

that the man who taught me how to ride a bike

is meant to spend his life in a cage.

Hurts like hell to watch you put your life on pause

like you don't got a daughter to raise.

I watched you grow from a pup into a wolf

more and more everyday.

This is your brother we're talking about.

He wrote letters talking about how

'I'll make it up to you when I come home, I promise'

And the letters they'll make no sense.

Girl, he said that shit to you too?

Yeah I know, they all do.

It's nothing new when you've heard it all before

from the men you thought were trustworthy.

How're you going to put us in a fucked up situation?

Do you know how many times

your daughter had to watch her mom cry?

How many times

your lil brother wish he had a man to look up to?

Now you the man who caused this effect.

Do you know how many hearts were broken in courtrooms?

Do you know bad it hurts?

To see your name written all over the news...

All because you were trapping out yo momma crib,

all because you pulled the trigger too many times,

all because you were out here finessing,

thinking you won't get finessed.

You could've just went home.

If you would have listened to the woman that was telling you so.

You could have saved yourself.

Cloud 9

You really can't take this life for granted.
I never knew this would be how things ended.
I was with you yesterday
when the sun came out to play.
We did everything.
Butterflies flying high now my skies are grey.
Like cloud 9, cloudy mind.
I got to find weather control.
I can't let you get a hold of me.
Even though I wish you were here holding me.
This isn't what it's supposed to be.
You were the best thing that ever happened to me
and I was your awakening.
We had a special kind of love.
That sing your heart out together type of love.
That 'I got your back' type of love.
That 'let me act right'.
That 'I don't have to fight back my love'
Man, I can't do this shit with nobody else but you.
But you've gone away...
Now I miss you like everyday.
So I pray that you're okay
wherever you are ...
Take care.

Lessons

Lessons I've learned:

- At some point in life, you will begin a spiritual journey and until then, you haven't really opened your eyes.
- Everything you need to know has already been shown to you, you have all the answers, dig deep within.
- Use your resources to the best of your ability, they are your steppingstones.
- In the end, it's all about family, whomever is family to you.
- Love is all you need.
- Music has the power to set the vibe in a room. Make sure the music you choose to be surrounded by is uplifting and not degrading.
- The more you take action in the moment, the more you'll thank yourself later.
- Travel the world as much as you can, there is so much to learn and see.
- Forgiveness is healing.
- Budgeting & investing will save your life.

Take Care

Are you still trying to get over the same things?
Do you know what healing really means?
Are you comfortable by yourself?
Or do you still need somebody's help?
Are you just trying to fill a void?
Are you ignoring your own voice?
I know you hear me but do you really feel me though?
How are you treating yourself?
How are you holding up these days?
Are you mindful of your health?
Are you saving your money?
Are you saving yourself?
Are you paying your karmic dues?
Are you taking care of you?
Did you clean your room?
Are you creating space?
Did you thank the sun?
Did you pray to the moon?
Did you come to an epiphany that it all starts with you?

Butterflies

Butterfly

I feel it coming.
I hear it calling my name.
I'm ready for change.
I'm going through the growing pains,
I'm working through a hard time
and sometimes I cry
cause I'm so blessed to be here.
Here where I can feel all the hues.
Feel all the sunshine and bad news.
I learned that you can be blue and still fly.
I know what it's like to die and still try.
That's the blessing in being alive.
You got to be friends with the monsters inside of your head.
Don't be afraid
when they got your back against the wall and you're ready to fall,
don't fold because I promise you got something to live for.
I know this is way out of your comfort zone,
but you got to learn not to get too comfortable.
Some say they don't recognize who I'm becoming.
Some days I don't recognize myself either.
But I love myself through it all.
The rise and the fall.
I might've left to get right but I'll be right back.
Better than I ever been.
I know I'm not for everybody.
But I'm thankful for those who call and check up on me.
Even when it's been a year and some change.
We're doing big things now.
I don't have time for the small talk.
I need keys for this and that
so I can open up some doors and I can put them on lock.

Are you catching my drift?
You really got to put the work in to see how it turns out.
On the way it won't be easy, but you'll be proud on the way out.
The journey of life is what this is all about.
First you earn your stripes, then you earn your wings...
Look mom I can fly!

Circle Of Life

The Indigenous people who are birthed on this land.
Home of your mother's mother, your father's father
and all the lovers who kept the generations growing
and so on because it goes way back.
Way back to notorious world wars,
way back to Gutenberg's Printing Press,
way back to the Renaissance Age,
way back to the Titanic and Pearl Harbor,
way back to the invention of the light bulb,
way back to Harriet Tubman, Rosa Parks and Sojourner Truth.
Way back to Malcolm X, MLK, and Nelson Mandela.
Way back to 2020 because *we made history.*
This is the story the kids will hear someday.
This is the story my ancestors brought me here to say.
The experiences of tragic events and the reward of being a warrior
who made it out alive. I have the honor to share this story.
It's these historical events that make us who we are today.
Because it's all so much bigger
than just you or a small-town girl like me.
We got spirits guiding us on different levels of existence.
So when we give thanks,
we must show our respect
to our beloved ancestors who have ascended.
It's important to dig deep and know your roots
so you can remember where you came from.
How lost is your body?
How many times has your spirit lived on?
Can you recognize that spirit over and over again?
The day my great grandmother died,
I held her hand and her spirit told me...
"I'll go everywhere you go"
from that day forward, she came to me as pretty birds.
Red meadowlark to be exact.

But also, as mourning doves
because she would always sing her blues to me.
And I would listen and try to match her rhythm.
My great grandmother was a holy woman.
She believed in something greater than her,
but she was always great to me.
Her cherry red nail polish matched the blood in the water
when I washed my hands after cleaning up my mess.
Cleaning up my act, trying to detach from generational curses.
Trying to learn from their mistakes.
Trying to unlearn the old programming.
Trying to be better than who raised me.
Trying to grow bigger than where I came from.

B.L.A.M.E

Dear black American girl, dear black American boy,
black lives always matter everywhere.
We are out here protesting in the streets,
fighting for our rights as humans in this capitalist society.
They're capping too much to make America great.
It's been this way since the beginning of civilization.
You're only a noble man
when you give back to the people of the land.
Don't be so selfish.
There's people less fortunate than what you flex for Instagram.
I know food stamps and a cup of noodles all too well.
I know hanging the clothes on the line and bucket baths all too well.
I know bare feet on concrete.
I know working 7 days a week isn't for the weak.
I know heating the house with the oven.
I know what it's like to have nothing.
I know the struggle of a single parent.
I know the struggle of trying your best.
I know when things go south,
you got to have the attitude of Kanye West.
My mother was a freedom fighter
trying to make her way in a man's world.
Because the way the system is set up, they don't want to see us win.
I grew up in the mud with my little brother
and I always told that nigga "The streets don't love you like I do"
so, when you've been gone for too long king, It starts to worry me.
Please answer your phone when you hear my ring
or please just come home to me.
Because I don't want to get a call with bad news.
I don't want to cry cause something happened to you.
I know some don't appreciate our melanin.
They tell us our hair is too nappy
and our features are too big and brown...

But they always love our culture.
They use us as entertainment.
Then they step on our necks.
But I'm wrong if I shoot back?
I'm wrong because I'm too black?
We cry and they laugh.
We don't deserve this.
How are we the ones to blame when
black lives always matter everywhere!
You should be the one in shame for treating us inhumane...
I know you never care...
But I am your neighbor.
I am your partner for the science project.
I am your favorite artist.
I am in the same line as you in the grocery store.
But you're all in a rush like we're trying to win a race...
No competition, get out of your own way.
Work at your own pace.
In real life, we all come from the same place.
And at the end of the day, we all want love...
So why am I still begging for justice on my brother's case?
Why is my sister walking around with mace?
It's sad that this world can't be a safe place.
So we stay armed and dangerous as our way of being safe.
But I want that to change.
I want to walk outside and it still feels like home
I don't want to feel like a target for just being myself.
I shouldn't feel so afraid of the world.
Because as a collective, we are one, we are human.
So, let's show some kindness!

Masquerade Party

You wear your mask to prevent illness.
You wear your mask but you're still sick in the mind.
You wear your mask but I can still see it in your eyes.
You wear your mask but your energy doesn't lie.
You wear your mask out of fear.
You wear your mask to hide the real you.
You wear your mask like it's supposed to save you.
You wear your mask but you're still the same you.
You wear your mask but you're no superhero.
You wear your mask and I hope it helps you sleep better at night.
You wear your mask so the show goes on and the party don't stop.
You wear your mask but you can take it off now.

Madness

Life is mad...
mad crazy, mad emotional, mad intense, mad passionate...
And sometimes in the madness, we get lost in the fire.
Because life can get wild when you're chasing the wind,
Just going with the flow, losing all control...
I know life moves so fast it can be blinding.
You just need some guidance.
Because direction is more important than speed.
So take your time, slow and steady.
Dip your feet in the water.
Is it just right? Do you like it like that?
Don't dive in head first.
You know better than to lose your mind
because you've been lost before.
Lost in the deep end but you swim good now.
Because you know what it's like to drown...
You know what it's like wearing your heart on your sleeve
and these days you know pain so well you wear it with ease.
You know how to say cheese when the cameras flashing
but that's only when the lights come on.
Only because you want the likes to go on...
So the show goes on...
Now you got a couple hearts
but where is your heart at?
What's the main attraction?
Where is the real love at?
Don't get too caught up.
Sometimes you got to fall back.
All to see the bigger picture.
What's sad is I never thought I had to cut you out.
Crazy how you can lose over the things you're most passionate about.
Life will trip you out like that. Make sure you don't go out so bad...

I'm just trying to find my way out of the bullshit.
Trying to find my way out of the madness.
My way out the matrix.
Maybe we're all too connected to the wrong things.
And we should disconnect, we should log off
Just to focus on our wellbeing.
Reconnect with something bigger, something better.
I'm thinking outside of the box because I ain't no square bitch.
Catch me outside of the box with my rings on.
I'm a savage and I know Victoria's secret.
Now they big mad because they want to be in my spot.
So they'll make stories up in their head
trying to hit me with their best shot.
The green in your pretty eyes isn't love, it's envy.
I see through it all but I don't let it phase me.
I know people go through personal things
and sometimes they come off ugly.
I know you're mad but we're all mad here.
Let the ambition of your madness encourage you
to march forward with a movement that finally
allows you to see the day where you know *peace*.

When Doves Cry

Mourning after mourning,
I wish someone could kiss my blues
and make me feel like ecstasy again.
But this pain sits too deep within my being.
Buried in the shadows,
I don't want to cry no more.
So, I write my blues and boy do they sound lovely...
Sounds like everything you wish
you could've said to me before we ran out of time.
Pretty bird, I hear your cries.
And Although it might seem so sad in your eyes,
on the bright side, I found your voice.
Your songs are soulful.
Seems like your songs are the only way you can reach me
when you can't pick up the phone.
But I know your calling when it hits home.
You told me you would get back to me.
You told me we would make it here eventually.
You told me no matter how it goes, make sure to live out the legacy.
And this isn't one of them stories you could play back.
So, I'm moving forward with the promise I made,
and nothing could change that.
I'm playing for keeps because it's been mine.
I just have to find my way...
So, when doves cry, I listen to the pretty birds.
I study the language of the universe.
So I can sing along, out loud
and write them down so you can read along...
Later, after my time runs out...
"Just follow the directions I gave you and you'll figure it out..."
you said.

Angel Baby

I spoke to god about you.
I told god I'd do my best for you.
I'd shelter you from the storm,
I'll make a home out of myself.
And I cried at the thought of miscarrying you...
I cried because I thought what if I'm not good enough?
And I thought what if I'm not built for this life?
What if life has other plans for me
and plan b is to meet you on the outside
because I can't hold you inside.
You're just the little boy I lock eyes with on the plane ride
or the little girl I meet when it's play time.
But one thing about you... we'll meet someday.
Whether it's now or next lifetime,
we'll meet at the right time.
And I'll you hold you in my arms, baby.
& little do I know, I need you
to show me how to hold somebody.
Because the way I've been held
will never compare to your hold on me.
Baby, the name I first gave you was love.
You are the greatest teacher, the greatest lover.
You are a star, you are my world.

Scandalous Lover

Last time I saw you we hugged and cried on your front porch.
I remember screaming
'you don't love me, you don't even love yourself.'
I saved your life so many times all for you to ruin mine...
I defended you when I shouldn't have.
I'm still trying to forgive me for loving you so deeply the way I did.
Both a blessing and a curse.
First you love it then it hurts.
Next comes the destruction of our own selves
for the love of the other.
Sacrificing all you've got for them.
Giving up your life or even your soul to please them.
In love so deep,
we honor it to the point where we will follow beloved
even into hell because what else more could we give?
What greater sacrifice is there?
It's 'anything for you, my love"
Shame on me, I should've watched my step.
Why did I ignore all the signs?
I seen everything that I didn't want to see.
I became somebody I didn't want to be.
You traumatized me.
I hope the world sees just who you are.
You are no angel.
You played the hero, but you really are the villain
I should've listened...
But I helped you fight your addiction.
Just to find myself fucked up and abused in the end...
Now I'm bigger than you so I can't meet you where you are.
I'd just be stunting my growth.
I should've left you alone
but I let you in my home and you infected me with your love.
But it'll all catch up to you eventually...

My bounce back will have you wishing you ain't fuck up so bad...

I hope you live happily ever after with her.
I hope she knows the deal you come with.
Wish I knew sooner...
We left off the same way we found each other.
Still broken, still healing.
Trying to make the pain go away,
thinking love will come and save the day
but I think we should save ourselves.
I pray you learn to love the boy within you.
I pray you find the man you were born to be.
I pray you face your demons, I pray you find your peace.

Over You

You thought you knew the game and ended up playing yourself.
You thought you could have your cake and eat it too
but you can't have her and her and her and have my love all for you.
You be lying baby and me too.
But I don't want to lie to keep you.
We both know that isn't true.
If that's the case I rather go my own way like I don't need you.
You thought I'd surrender myself to protect you,
so you can go have your fun while the girls cry.
The girls never cried for you,
the girls cried because look at the fucking mess you made
and you don't care to clean up.
But here I am trying not to cry over spilt milk.
I'm not your wifey or your baby momma,
I don't need that drama.
I could be a lone wolf.
You know I'm miss independent.
You can't catch this flight with me,
you're not part of my ascension.
Look at the present we get from this ending.
I hope you take time for yourself to do some reflecting.
I hope you see the pain you caused.
I hope you see where you went wrong.
No more partying with teenage girls.
Fuck your fantasy.
I'm a grown ass woman.
Learn how to handle me.
I don't want to wonder why you're acting shady.
Why you ain't been calling me 'baby'.
You aren't acting like the man for me,
maybe cause you got another lady.
I know I shouldn't stay for another day...

But every time I'm with you I don't want to behave.
But how can you blame me?
Look at the woman you made of me...
You put me on game and now I'm running with it
running ... over you.

Miss Jackson

I'm sorry miss Jackson but I had to leave your son.
You don't know how he was acting...
If you knew what happened behind closed doors,
you'd tell me to run.
He played me like videogames he thought I was just fun.
And I thought he was the one.
Maybe I was just young.
Nineteen and way too deep in love
that I forgot about me.
Me and your son we were great but he's just not what I need.
But I thank him for teaching me everything I know now.
At a time, it was perfect, but I have to go now.
I'm sorry miss Jackson but I had to leave your son.
Thankyou for giving me a best friend in your incredible son
but your boy just isn't the one for me.
A girl gets tired of the hoes and the lies,
hoping it'll get better next time...
But I need a man this time.
A man who only sees me
and wouldn't jeopardize our bond for anybody.
I know this is your son we're talking about
and you'll always have his back.
I just wish you didn't look at me so badly
because what he tells you is really all cap.
I was the girl who was there at his lows.
I was the girl who went and supported his shows.
I was the girl who he had before everything.
I was the girl who was supposed to make him a family guy...
& I was also the girl he didn't see in his future.

Grieve

Sometimes we lose people in life
and we don't ever really heal from it.
Time just passes us by and we learn how to wear pain better.
But behind closed doors I know you.
I know you fall to your knees asking
'why god? Why couldn't I go, too?"
I know how bad it hurts you.
I know how traumatizing it can be.
I know you can't put a time on how long you grieve.
You just feel it all...
Trying to detach from it all...
Give me my space.
I am not okay.
But "I'm fine" I say.
I'll find my way... to live without you.

21 Questions

Am I moving too slow or too fast for you?
Am I doing the most or not enough?
Did I ever let my ego talk too loud?
Am I too aggressive for you?
Am I overprotective with my love?
Did I care too much?
Did I think too deep?
Did I think too far ahead?
Is my love too passionate?
Are my standards too high?
Am I worth taking a chance with?
Am I worth settling for?
Am I the one you want to bring home to your mother?
Am I the one you want to build a life with?
Am I selfish for focusing on me this time?
Am I selfish for putting priorities before play?
Am I really crazy for calling you out on your bullshit?
Am I crazy for calling you at all?
Did I hurt your feelings the way I let it go?
Did I hurt your feelings the way I moved on my own?

Can You Be The One?

I'm not for everybody.
Some days I want to be left alone,
somedays I want to be shown some love.
Somedays I'm sweet, somedays I'm savage.
Somedays I got it all, somedays I lose my balance.
It takes a real one to deal with a woman like me.
But I promise I'm worth it.
To be loved by a worthy man.
I will show you my love and my hands.
I want you to know I come in honesty.
Can you match my energy?
I want my presence craved anytime I go missing.
I want my spirit full in return of me giving my everything.
I just want somebody who sees me for who I am, authentically.
Can you laugh with me and play in my fantasy?
Then bring me back down to earth and remind me of reality?
I want somebody who can keep their cool
and never lose their patience with me.
Somebody who was raised to know loyalty.
I want to wake up to an unconditional lover.
I crave a love so intimate I just want you in my space.
I want a love I don't have to chase.
I want to love and be loved so loud
that we don't have to question 'what is this?'
We know our love is bold and please don't ever let it get cold.
Because for my love, I need the fire.

Love Me Like You Say

If you love me like you say you do, would you ride for me?
If you love me like you say you do, would you be blood about it?
If you love me like you say you do, would you be loyal no matter the conditions?
If you love me like you say you do, would you love me behind my back?
If you love me like you say you do, would you scream it to the world?
If you love me like you say you do, would you teach me how to play?
If you love me like you say you do, would you shield my name?
If you love me like you say you do, would you feel my pain?
If you love me like you say you do, would you show me your love?

Cherish the Moment

Can we never mind the titles, the expectations, the drama?
Getting too caught up in what this is supposed to be,
Instead of just being here with me.
Can we value our time more?
Are the games still exciting?
Don't you wanna put your control down and slow down...
Can we just have fun now?
Let's enjoy the weather while the suns out.
Let's never mind the what if's, the potential, the fantasy.
Let's enjoy each others company
I want you to make me feel like I'm the only girl in the world
because I want to make you feel like you're the only man.
Let's make this love run deep,
beyond our time...
Like 50 summers later even when the sun don't shine.
Let's make it a story worth telling.
All because we cherished the moment.

Between Us

Can you keep it between you and I?
What's between us is nobody's business.
Honestly, what's between us anyways?
Is it distance? Is it dark secrets?
Is it a closed door? Is it somebody else?
Or is it your own ego
that holds your pride so high,
you wouldn't dare jump off your high horse
for a moment of silence or for a simple fucking thank you.
Yet you tell me 'the only thing between us is love'
So, if you call this love then tell me
how much trust is there between us?
How much loyalty is there beyond us?
How many years must we put between us
to prove this is a forever thing?
And if things change,
tell me how many years must we put between us to prove
love no longer lives here?
How many bittersweet Novembers?
How many summers?
How deep will you ride to keep the love between us?

Everlasting

I love you beyond measure.
I love you a thousand miles away.
I will love you until we're old and grey.
I want to become ghosts with you.
I want to help you love life into the next time.
And I promise to always have the patience that love demands.
I know my heart will break over and over again
because that's just what life comes with.
But your love makes it easier to keep going.
I love the smell of your cologne on the sheets.
I love the smell of the roses you bring.
I love the way you inspire me to be better.
It's something about your demeanor.
Something about the way you move so graciously.
Something about your charisma and your ambition.
And I absolutely love the way you see the world.
That makes you different from the others.
Because you my love, are outstanding.
That made you to be my chosen one.
And I love you for seeing me in that same light.
You are a star in my eyes.
Thank you.
Thank you for always being so supportive of me.
Thank you for dinner.
Thank you for the flowers.
Thank you for the massage and long talks.
Thank you for listening.
Thank you for understanding me when my words fall short.
Thank you for trying to find new ways to love me better.
Thank you for showing me what real love is.

Where The Magic Begins

I write without knowing who my words will find.
But I know I found myself right here.
Here, where I'm unafraid to lay my heart on the line
when my heart grows too heavy to hold.
From the depths of my sorrows to the highest of heights.
I write without dreams of awards or an applause.
I don't need a standing ovation or for folks to fall at my feet.
I know my superpower and I'm using this little light of mine
to let you know there's a way for us all.
It doesn't matter who or what tries to steer you off your path,
your soul knows it's purpose and that is your superpower.
When the light dims, find your spark again.
Ask yourself...
''what is that keeps me in alignment with my soul's purpose?''
Whatever answer feels right, do just that.
The magic begins when you listen to your intuition,
direct your thoughts and execute your masterplan.

GCODE Pt.2 (The Game)

The game of life is a wild card.
Make the best out of the hand that you're dealt.
And remember not to deal with the bullshit,
you don't deserve that.
Haters watching from the sidelines
will always try to knock you down.
It's usually the ones from the same area code.
But stick to the GCODE.
Play defense, keep your guard up.
Block the ex men, block the small minded bitches.
All of them are way out of your league.
Keep your head in the game.
Ball like Kobe,
give yourself a name.
I shoot my shot and I don't ever miss.
Even my losses are lessons learned.
I just make it look so effortless.
Hoops in, real big,
rings on like I already won the championship.
I'm balling like the March Madness.
You can be a player, but I'll always be the coach.
Now I'm going to pass the ball to my teammate
just to give them a shot.
Whole team already ate I just want to see what they got.
2 points from me, 2 points from you.
You got to make sure the people in your circle adding it up too
or else they're going to fuck around and take it all from you.
Tell them get they own.
I'm too grown to be played with.

So, there they go switching sides,
trying to play for the other team thinking the grass greener.
That's a personal foul.
I'm speaking in code but maybe I should get personal now.
Cause the way you played me you got cut off, timeout.
Don't violate me when the ball is in my court.
Don't think you're the game changer when I'm the star,
you're going to fall short...
I'm the real MVP they could never ever bench me.
I'm making a few points here...
When it's my time to shine, I'm going to own that year.
I really started from the bottom
now I'm on my way up.
Practice makes perfect.
So, I'm mastering the game
and they're clocking my movements.
I don't do challenges cause my only competition is me myself and I.
I don't play with them cause my aim is too high
and we don't see eye to eye.
And certain moves they make I ain't cool with so I pass that
cause I'm past that.
I let that shit slide.
I'm ahead of my time.
GCODE is really the cheat code.
There's levels to this shit
and you just found one of the keys.
Now that it's unlocked, I'm going to reload...

Listen to The Music

If you're ever wondering if I write about you, I do.
I don't have to say your name. You know it's you.
Even though it isn't about us no more. You are still my muse.
How could I let you die like that?
Letter after letter I write you
but I don't ever hear back...
Sometimes when I listen closely, I can still hear your laugh.
I still smell you here.
The ghost of you still lingers around...
And I ask why won't you go away for good?
Don't you want to rest in peace?
Spirit screams back at me 'sometimes I feel so alive I can't sleep'
Sometimes my passion keeps me up past 2
Letter after letter I write you...
You always show up through my words.
Maybe this is your way of living with me forever.
Maybe all I ever have to do is listen closely.
Listening to the music as I slow dance in my apartment.
Spirit sings "here is where you'll always find me."

One Time

If it's one thing for sure, it's that I'll always love you.
Too many lovely people, too many unforgettable moments.
Third, just know everything will be okay.
When it comes fourth, I'll have your back no matter what.
On my whole hand, I count how many years it has been & I keep on...
Six is the golden hour.
Seven is when the sun sets.
Eight is for infinity and beyond.
Nine, I hope you're ready.
By the end, the alarm goes off, your flight takes off and time is up.
Now you're back at the one time and make sure it's a good time.
Because years go by too fast...

Wishing Well

I hope you're enjoying your day.
I hope you're finding your way.
I understand people aren't meant to stay and that's okay.
We come and we go,
we learn and we grow.
You're either going to ride or die.
I just hope we impact each other's lives for the better.
I hope you get all that you deserve.
And I hope you still think of me when our song plays
and smile back at those good days
and remember It's still a good day
even when you leave people in yesterday.
Feels like just yesterday we were watching the sunset in Brooklyn.
Feels like just yesterday we were swimming at 4am in Mexico.
Feels like it was us against the world
and now it's like I don't even know who you are anymore.
We always talked about growing old together but we died young.
All that just to give you a woman to remember...
I still see you in my dreams.
This time we went to Greece.
I don't know what that means
but I want to keep the peace
no matter how much space we got in between.
Cheers to growing up with me.
Too bad we didn't get to see past 21.
I guess we aren't on the same quest no more.
Things changed and our missions aren't the same.
I'm sorry it turned out this way but we move different now.
You don't seem to care much but I do.
I had to swallow my pride just to say happy birthday to you.
It's cool, I get it...
We don't talk anymore but here's a penny for your thoughts.
I wish you well.

The Last Dance

Our last dance was at the dance recital in 2009
Our last dance was at my sweet 16
Our last dance was at prom
Our last dance was at the graduation party
Our last dance was at the club downtown
Our last dance was at the wedding
Our last dance was at that house party
Our last dance was the first time we ever danced
Our last dance was the last time you held me that close
If we get the chance to dance again,
I'll play a song that'll never end...

The Last Songs

The Book Of Soul

I write for men and women.

I write for people of color.

For adolescents coming of age.

Depression.

I write for freedom.

For ecstasy.

I write for bad days and the best times of our lives.

With love, for love.

From me, too you.

My legacy.

Feels

Is there anything left to feel?
I think I've been through it all.
From pure bliss to envious bitterness,
High in love to fallen.
Yet let's not forget, sweet, idealistic hope.
So hypnotizing it takes you to the edge of the world.
Reminding you that there is always more to feel.
But nothing will ever come close to what has been felt
because you'll never feel the same twice.

Room 714

I went to the party that night and there you were.
We locked eyes and I saw sparks fly like the 4th of July.
But it was October when me and my friends came over.
'Who's the girl with the curly hair" you told her,
pointing over at me.
The whole night you were aiming for me.
Then we had some time alone on the balcony
and you couldn't stop talking about the city
and how I'm so pretty.
We were just strangers who became a little more than friends.
That one night turned into every weekend
and now we chillin' like every evening
and I'm thinking...
Who would have known it would get this far?
Who would have known it would end this soon?
Feels like yesterday when I met you.
How could I forget you?
What if I told you that forever is a moment
when time doesn't exist.
Would you have kept it for the moment?
or still have taken the risk of taking it deeper than this?
You see, nobody was searching for anybody.
Just travelers who so happened to cross paths
and it happened so fast...

But I know the universe did this on purpose.
Nothing is coincidental.
Ever since then I always kept it on my mental...

What if the key to this journey
was to find the most value within ourselves
upon meeting each other?
What if that is the treasure we get to keep from one another?
Or what if I would've left you at the party and closed the door?
What if it was just that and nothing more?

Guns & Roses

While we were together,
I felt you used me because you needed me.
Needed me for your sanity.
I was a place of peace for you.
But I had to leave you at the crossroads.
I hope you understand why it was time to go.
Now things have changed, I don't see you the same.
I'm tired of not being happy with you.
I'm tired of not being happy with myself.
We don't have to stay and play guns and roses.
Shit isn't sweet, it's hopeless.
It isn't all grapes and wine,
just thorns and vines.
This is a losing game in time.
I never understood how you always wanted to grow
but never willing to change.
I guess it was the growing pains
that had you in chains.
So now we're growing apart.
Cheers to a new start.
While you're at a standstill, I'm evolving.
You weren't meant to come with me.
This is the end of this chapter.
Nice to meet you, I'm sorry I can't stay.

Smooth Criminal

Mind games and manipulation,
you can keep that shit over there.
Talking all that sugar-coated sweet shit
but it's real gangsta over here.
Tell me how it tastes when you see me walking away...
Away from you, I still remember those days.
These days it hurts to look you in the face,
to be reminded of such a place.
Like you never been apart of my pain,
like you never lied to my face,
like you never made it rain.
Now you expect me to act like it's all good?
Man, tell your lawyer I ain't paying shit
cause your talk is cheap and I ain't buying it.
Wasted times, that should've been mine.
So this is payback and I hope you feel that.

Call Me

Call me mad
Call me crazy
Call me sad
Call me on a late night
Call me when you need, my love
Call me by my name
Call me out on my bullshit
Call me out of my mind
Call me when you have time
Call me when you get home
Call me when you see this
& when I call you, you better answer

Fly Woman

I'm too good for all this shit.

I don't belong here to put up with it.

I just wanna be a fly woman.

So don't hold me down.

You can't keep me around

to be the company for your misery

because love is free.

So just let me be... a fly woman.

Thank you for not stopping me on my way out.

You kept me going...

You told me the world is mine

so I'm going to own it.

Like I control the party.

So Far & Close

We took it too far.
Now we're too far from where we started.
Never thought it'd get like this.
Never thought it'd be you that I miss
You haunt everything that I know
but somehow it makes you feel closer...
Closer to me.
Wondering how you're taking this cause I'm too far...
Far from you.
Trying not to worry too much about wherever you are.
I got to get back to me.
I'm here trying to love my space.
Trying to get back into shape
cause you had me bent.
We should've never taken it too far.
But everything happens for a reason.
Reason why I'm far from you and closer to me.
You say "go on girl, make me so proud.
I'll stay so far if that means being closer to you.
Your exclusiveness is desirable.
So go ahead and do it big like you should girl,
do it how they never thought you could girl."

So I'm going to take it so far.
Far from where we started.
Never thought it'd get like this.
Never thought I would flip the script.
Now it's me that you miss.
& this is as close as it gets...

One Love

We get our hearts broken

then go breaks hearts the same way we were taught...

How to love?

Where's the love when we're broken apart

by the same thing that brings us together...

Love hurts, but it's the pain that brings pleasure.

Pictures

Remember In the past when we spoke about our future?

We painted a picture of our lives and what it could've been.

You told me you'd always and forever be my best friend

and love me until the very end.

In your own ways you did.

But the hardest part is you had to break my heart too.

And to find my way, I had to lose you.

I guess we only painted the picture in vibrant hues.

We must've forgotten about the black and blues.

But if you're ever wondering about me,

the picture we painted is still hung in my room...

I haven't forgotten about you.

I haven't forgotten about the time when we were younger,

and you told me "Only time can tell"

Now were years deep and time revealed the bigger picture.

Maybe after all, you weren't meant to fit the frame.

Just a moment in time when you made me laugh.

Now I don't want to be stuck in the past

but here I am crying over pictures and old photographs.

28

I know you would have never thought I'd be the one.
The one to shatter your heart in two million pieces.
That was never my intention
but you never fail to mention,
that I wasn't just another "fish in the sea".
You said "You're a goldfish, Ki"
For all the lessons I bring, I hope you learned something.
Despite everything,
you make it known
that you have a special place in your heart for me.
So my apologizes for walking out on you so elegantly.
Like I just kept it moving, like it didn't hurt me.
Truth is, it hurts like hell to stay and destroy me.
So I let go so I could stop bleeding in love.
Just know I needed your love.
You know I have my reasons...
If we meet again, then I'll know the meaning
four all of the seasons.
We'll both be great like twenty eighty-eight, you say.
But baby, we've got to separate
to dedicate this love to ourselves.
Although it hurts like hell,
time will show and tell.
I love you but I have to go now...

Wandering Star

When the day is done and I lay me down,

I lay alone without you around.

I look up to the sky and pray to a star so bright.

I told them dig graves for two.

I don't want to live a life without you.

I think about the vows we made,

It makes me sad you've gone away...

Why'd you have to leave so soon?

Oh, what a life we're born to.

This is no promise land.

Off of the face of the earth,

you're off to neverland...

To the undiscovered place which we know not of.

A place where no traveler returns from.

Wandering star,

I know you're free wherever you are.

I feel your ghost,

I know you're close.

Maybe I'll get to see you again next lifetime...

Only God knows the right time

in this infinite lifeline...

Happy Birthday

When Gaia calls me home
to the garden of Eden,
celebrate this life of mine
with sweet wine, higher than cloud 9.
& if I die before I wake,
celebrate this life of mine
so happy for heaven's sake.
Bake me a cake and sing happy songs.
No trail of tears.
I'm where I belong.
Freedom at last, when we say goodbye to earth.

Soulmates

Like déjà vu, I've been here with you in another atmosphere.
We crossed roads,
I felt this spirit before.
I feel your energy near, even light years away...
This feels like home,
this feels like something I've always known.
We're two of a kind and when the stars align,
you're my parallel.
You've shown me my truest self.
Out of body,
we've got soul ties.
We vibe on the same frequency.
You match my energy.
You compliment me.
You get me soul high.
I don't want to come down.
So, tell me what this is now?
This is deeper than love.
Checkmate, I found my soulmate.
This feels so great, the greatest of all time...
Soul long.

The Last Day Of Summer

The sun is beaming when we wake up.

The birds are singing as we pack up all of our belongings.

Kiss me hard before you go...

On with the day in our own ways

but we never broke up.

Just space to say 'i miss you'.

It hurt so bad I cried on the bathroom floor.

It was a sad day without you.

I wanted more...

Time with you is always sacred.

Time without you is what I make it.

So I'm going to make it something amazing.

We never broke up.

Life separated us.

No love lost.

They can't take my love away,

my love for you is here to stay.

But I'll go on and enjoy my day,

no tears left to cry.

I'll be okay without you by my side.

We never broke up we just never kept in touch.

I can't remember

the last time we asked how our days have been.

Days without her, days without him...

I just wanted to say thank you for being a part of my journey.

You taught me patience

that led me to greatness and now I'm so amazing

Even when I'm out having the time of my life

with my friends in the city,

I still wish you were here to do it with me.

I think about you everyday.

It's 4 in the morning and I can't help but to think

of the times when we laughed and loved,

cried and hugged.

I'll never forget where I came from.

My pain will always have your name on it

and for you I am so thankful.

Now this summer's over

and we're watching the sun finally set.

I Love You

I wouldn't be who I am without you.

You taught me how to fight,

both with my hands and mentally.

You taught me how to be bold

and live a life that's meant for me.

You taught me how to be a warrior.

You made me laugh so hard I'd cry.

You shown me bravery through tragedy.

You taught me how to love unconditionally and infinitely.

Thank you, for being everything that you are.

I truly do adore you.

You are such a star.

More than honored to be a reflection of who you are.

Flower Girl

You planted every seed
inside of me
all to watch me
grow without you.
Aren't you so proud to see
The woman that I've blossomed to?

Vixen

I am her, the woman who ran with the wolves.

We howl at the same moon when day is dusk.

We listen to the night calls,

we rendezvous at nightfall,

under the moon like the night ball.

He gazes at me dancing in my little black dress.

Admiring my dominance as I dance with the devil in elegance.

Careful now, you better watch your step.

But I follow the rhythm to my own heartbeat.

I follow my intuition, it always takes the lead.

I am still a holy woman even on nights I sin.

Then I pray to my God that they don't prey on me.

Oh my God, please don't ever leave me.

Don't feed me to the wolves because they would eat me.

Down to the bone, I've got skeletons in my closet

from my past lives I've lived.

Born again like I got nine lives to live.

I was raised to be ready by ten.

I was raised to be ready alone.

Even when I thought it was us against them.

Only I, from the beginning to the end.

I am her, the woman who runs it.

Perdoname

I've forgiven you for the nights you didn't come home.

For the nights I cried myself to sleep.

For the days I didn't eat

cause the knot in the back of my throat

couldn't even let me speak.

I don't know why I let you in

when I should've left you to beg on your knees.

But I've forgiven you for the sake of me.

But please, forgive me too.

For the times I screwed up acting like a fool.

Acting like I don't have nothing to lose.

For the shit I put you through...

Forgive me for the sake of you.

Home

Running back to our sanctuary to restore the connection.

You recognize yourself when you see me
cause I'm your reflection.

I gave you an arrow and you put me through it.

Shot me like cupid, I'm so stupid to let you do it.

You struck me to the core of my being.

My heart, you know how to make me breathe different.

You touch me in places I'm the most insecure.

You kiss my knees and my shoulders.

You remind me that I'm yours.

This feels like my cure.

You listen to me even when you don't understand.

You always held my hand.

You hold me like I'm worshipped.

Nobody sees that side of me,

inside of me, like soul deep, confide with me.

Do you know what that feels like?

To actually be kissed by the sun?

To be on a level like this is not something ordinary.

Studies of our beauty marks, scars,

our eyes, the sighs, the nights we lied with just the vibe...

Tell me that isn't love.

Tell me what you're fearful of.

Give it to me raw and tell me what you need from love.

Love, I can be your home to come to.

The Wanderer

Hey, my apologies for running away how I did...

I'm on a quest to find what's best, for me.

So please, don't go searching, I'm okay.

I love you but I just needed to get away.

To be in my own space,

in a place where the wild things are.

I can't promise I won't wander too far...

But I'll be sure to return with treasure of some sort.

With more than I left with, that's for sure.

I've been working overtime.

Trying to keep focus on my grind, my craft, my mind.

This takes practice.

No distractions.

No days off.

Just me getting lost...

All to find exactly what I've been looking for.

My Beautiful Dark Twisted Fantasy

Life is a fantasy and a nightmare all in one.

I'm so appalled by this power.

Who will survive in America?

It's one hell of a life.

I won't play the blame game.

I'll just run away to my dark fantasy.

Say hello to ecstasy.

See me now,

devil in a new dress.

They call me the gorgeous monster.

The way I prosper led me...

To all of the lights.

Preach

Thank you, everyday.
For being by my side.
For showing me the signs.
For giving me insight.
For bringing the truth to the light.
I pray you continually bless me
in ways I can't even begin to describe
how thankful I am.
Go on protecting my energy and my aura,
my people, and all that I love.
I pray you bless me with the power of love,
strength, wisdom, courage and abundance
to go on...
Even when the world feels like it's caving in on me...
To go on...
Being the best I can be.
To preach, to teach, and learn a life of love.
To speak when you're afraid.
To move when I feel dead inside.
To believe when I don't feel alive.
Take good care.
Guide me when I lose balance.

My intuition.
My God.
My holy spirit.
My angels.
I vow to speak my truths,
value my worth,
and never lose sight of the bigger picture.
Harvesting positive thoughts
and detoxing negative vibes.
May god be with us,
Amen.

Dear Young Queen

Dear young queen, build your home while you're still young.

No worries, you'll have your time to have fun.

The party never ends.

But hard work will pay the bills before any cheap thrills.

So, build your home.

Not with sticks or stones but with something solid.

Don't let the wind or the wolves knock it.

Focus.

Build your home, a place to call your own.

A space to place all your trophies.

Make sure it's secured.

Before you let that man in.

Before you decide to have kids.

Build your home.

Even if you're all alone.

It won't be easy.

But even when you're blue inside,

make sure your sapphire is glistening.

Keep on building.

After all, dear young queen,

you'll have everything you ever dreamed of.

So build your home, before all else.

20-17

As a young girl, naive and free, not worried about a thing.
She did not see what was coming.
Only after the passage of time,
now a wise woman does she see it all.
The mistakes, the fake, the loss and close calls.
Everything she was oblivious to.
Because the youth in her spent years waiting, wanting, wishing.
Fucked up on stupid shit, too lit to realize the truth in it.
So here she is years in, experienced enough to say...
She was cluelessly on her way.
I wish I could have warned her
of the monsters and detours,
and the bullshit she will run into.
I wish I could have protected her
but I trusted her to take the long way home.
She figured it out on her own.
She could've turned out to be anybody
but she turned out to be you.
& girl, you turned out to be absolute.

Miss Ecstasy

Miss ecstasy, the girl of my dreams.

I fell in love with this woman.

Everything about her is so elegant.

I knew she'd be big as Madonna.

She got style like Rihanna.

Versace, Chanel and that Dolce and Gabbana.

She makes it seem so effortless because of her confidence.

She's fearless.

I admire that about her.

She has all the jazz.

Her wisdom made her best moves.

It's always chess with her,

she ain't ever let nobody check her.

She intrigues me.

Her aura is so dope.

She's my favorite person to be around.

She has a holy spirit.

I see the God in her.

I fell in love with her,

myself.

Create Reality

Let's go on a trip.
Let's get away this weekend.
Let's travel the world.
Say hello, New York City, Philly, Bali, London, Tokyo, Toronto
& all the beautiful places we can go.
On the run from the everyday hustle.
Fuck the everyday struggles.
The troubles, I don't fumble,
maybe trip, but I survive the jungle.
Get money and stay humble.
We do this like we already won.
Girls just wanna have fun.
All night, up till sunrise ,
orange skies,
making love under pretty lights.
So lit, a moment for life.
Let's snap another photograph of us all around the map.
When they ask 'how you do that?'
I tell them I worked so hard just to get the payback.
I really wanted the life I envisioned so I couldn't just lay back.
You just got to wake up and go get it.
If you want it, you can live it.
After a long night of dreaming,
up all night until the morning light,
plotting and scheming.
I can't believe what I'm seeing...
Who would have thought I'd wake up dreaming.

Sage

No strings attached, I cut the cords.

I sage my space,

I said my grace.

Now I'm on my way.

Rehab

On the first page of our story everything seemed so perfect.
Now why do I feel like this?
You don't even recognize what you're doing to me.
You must not care that this is so unhealthy.
Overdosing on ecstasy...
You can't even look at me.
Caught up in the thrill of it
and it gives me chills a bit... just the thought of it.
I guess that's what I get for wishful thinking.
You were too good to be true, you had ecstasy and all the blues.
Can't believe I had no clue.
I went through hell and back for you.
You were my lover and my best friend.
But deep in my heart I had feeling...
Feelings for you, feeling like this is something we shouldn't do
cause it always ends with one of the two...
And I don't want to lose you, I don't want to fight you,
I don't really hate you because I truly love you.
Can't you see that?
So don't pull back.
Don't tell me that you love it like that.
Don't tell me 'who cares when it feels like crack'
Cause this is bad, bad, bad, bad, bad.
You should go to rehab.
Go and get yourself back.
Then tell me who do you love? Is it me or the drugs?

Higher Self Speaking

Hey, you, I'm writing this letter to let you know you're going to fall in love

and it won't be so pretty. It'll strike you like lightning out of the blue.

You will get your heartbroken and although it may feel awful,

it won't kill you.

Tell your mother even though It'll frighten her.

Tell her that you love him so much,

that for once in your life, you're at a loss for words.

But that's okay because he's the reason your writing this anyways.

Now you can't seem to shut up about the shit you been through

cause you know that's what really made you.

But let's not be late for work again.

That job you're working at will feel like slavery for the bare minimum.

But I promise you won't ever be hungry or homeless.

It's just something to hold you down for the moment.

Something to feed your goals and wherever you're trying to go.

You'll trip but no worries, you won't fail. You just got to keep going...

You know you're going to make something

real inspirational with that talent.

Somebody the kids will look up to.

Somebody them boys wish they can have

and those girls wish they could be like.

You know you want to be that somebody.

If only they knew what it took.

The challenge of going beyond yourself to really know your strength.

Some days it took everything in you to keep going...

Because you know how many people try to shoot you down on the way up?
Distracting you from your main focus like 'hey wanna link up?'

It's the weekend, party starts at nine
but I think tonight I'm going to stay inside.
At first nobody will see your vision.
They'll tell you "You're lame, you should've came"
They'll tell you to go to school and be more "realistic".
But no dream is too big to not live. So live your fantasy.
Everyone else will follow up eventually.
You're going to master your talent.
You're going to become the girl of your dreams someday. Just be patient.
You have no idea the things coming your way are about to change your life.
If you knew what they were, you'd forgive yourself
for the way you thought it was never enough.
Because here you are doing the most.
I'm proud of you kid, it all turned out in your favor. You did it.

To you, Sincerely Me

Last but not least, thankyou.

You did this.

Thank you, for breaking my heart in the way that I needed.

Thank you, for reminding me of my superpowers.

You allowed me to overcome

everything I thought I couldn't conquer.

You allowed me to believe when I thought it wasn't true.

When I thought it wasn't you.

You encouraged me to find myself and I found you.

Somewhere along the way...

I'm so glad you came.

You came through for a reason.

I'm so glad you listened.

I'm so glad it worked out in our favor.

You are my favorite.

even when I hate it.

We found a way to make it.

Sometimes the way to get in, is with out.

Sometimes you have to take a different route.

But no matter what, trust god's plan without a doubt.

And last but not least, I'm sorry.

If I ever fell short.

If I ever broke your heart.

I'm sorry if I wasn't enough for you.

Or if I'm not who you thought I should be.

I'm sorry I can't be her

because I'm unapologetically me.

And you were too blind to see

the queen I was born to be.

So I'm sorry, I'm not sorry.

But if it was ever my fault, forgive me.

We live and we learn.

We give and we earn.

Seems like we had our fair share.

I'm sorry if I couldn't thank you enough

for being such an influence on how I made it here.

I made it here and I'm so proud of you, my dear.

Soundtrack To My Life:

J.Cole – Apparently
Jhene Aiko – Psilocybin, H.O.E, 10K Hours, Sativa,
Wading, Bed Peace
Majid Jordan- What You Do to Me, Something About You,
Gave Your Love Away
Lauryn Hill – Miseducation album
Frank Ocean – Channel Orange album
Travis Scott- Days Before Rodeo, Rodeo album
Kid Cudi -Pursuit of Happiness, Mr. Rager, Frequency, By Design
Justin Timberlake - Mirrors
Mary J Blige - Be Without You
Lady Antebellum- Need You Now, Just a Kiss
Adele- Someone Like You, Set Fire To The Rain,
Rolling Deep, Chasing Pavements
Queen Naija- Butterflies
Ariana Grande- Everyday, Successful, God is a Woman, Monopoly
Ciara – Goodies Album
Destiny's Child - Soldier
Future- Neva end, DS2 Album, Codeine Crazy
Gnarls Barkley- Crazy
Gwen Stefani- The Sweet Escape, Hollaback Girl, Rich Girl
Katy Perry- Last Friday night, The One That Got Away
The Weeknd- Trilogy
Partynextdoor- Options, Recognize, Make A Mill,
Partymobile album, Peace of Mind, Only U
Lana Del Rey- Summertime sadness, Blue jeans
Papikeepitrill- Painkillers

Beyonce- Love On Top, Upgrade U, Drunk In Love, Mine,
Rocket, Best Thing I Never Had
Daddy Lessons, All Night
Kanye West- Ultralight Beam, Blood on the leaves,
Love Lockdown, MBDTF, Ye,
No Church In The Wild, Niggas In Paris, Gotta Have It,
Who Gon Stop Me, Hold My Liquor, I'm In It, Slow Jamz
The Neighborhood- Wiped Out Album, Sweater Weather
Post Malone- Stoney album
Rick Ross - Aston Martin Music
Keyshia Cole- Just Like You album, The Way It Is Album,
Take Me Away, Last Night, Let It Go
Rihanna – LOUD, Talk That Talk, Anti album, BBHMM
Schoolboy Q- Studio, His and Her Fiend, Work Remix, THat Part,
Man Of The Year, Die Wit Em, Gangsta, Situations,
Hands On the Wheel
6lack- Balenciaga Challenge
Sza- CTRL Album, Good Days
Tink- No Hesitation, Jupiter, I like, Litty Again,
Cut It Out, Bottom Bitch, CAP, Rush
Willow- Female Energy, Ardipithecus Album
Kehlani- SexySexySavage Album,
It Was Good Until It Wasn't Album
XXXTENTACION- Fuck Love, NUMB, Moonlight, Ecstasy,
$$$, Going Down!
G Herbo - On My Soul, Kill Shit, At The Light, PTSD
Summer Walker- Over It Album
Trippie Redd- Till The End Of Time, Excitement,
Weeeeee, Never Change
Doja Cat- Roll With Us, Casual, Morning Light, Candy,
Boss Bitch, Bottom Bitch, Better Than Me

Pusha T- Sweet Serenade, Numbers On The Board, Nosetalgia
Dreezy- Spar, Distant Lover, Ecstasy
Chance The Rapper- Acid Rap Mixtape
Childish Gambino- Redbone, Heartbeat, 3005
Space Jesus - Dragonhawks, Sunrize, Professor Genius
Three Days Grace- Riot, Animal I have become, IHEAY
Aboogie- I Still Think About You, Jungle
Ab-Soul- Control System Album
Big Sean- Dark Sky Paradise Album, Time In
A$AP Rocky- LSD, LPFJ2, Fashion Killa, Wild For The Night, Goldie
Bryson Tiller- Trapsoul Album
Lady Gaga- Million Reasons, LoveGame, Paparazzi
Sia- Bird Set Free, Cheap Thrills
Drake – Jaded, Make Me Proud, Best I Ever Had, Losses,
Controlla, Legend, Madonna, Own It, Pound Cake,
Up All Night, Emotionless, What A Time To Be live Album
Justin Bieber- Baby, Stuck In The Moment, Runaway Love,
Somebody to Love
YoungAsh- Wine on Me
Lil Uzi- Super Saiyan, Top, Paradise, You Was Right,
Money Longer, Do I What I Want,
POP, Drankin' N Smokin', Marni On Me
Mac Miller- Weekend
Luther Vandross- Dance With My Father
Chris Brown- Forever, Strip, Go Crazy, No Guidance
Meek Mill- 1942 Flows, Dreams & Nightmares, Amen, Going Bad
Nicki Minaj- Buy A Heart, Moment 4 Life
Ari Lennox- Shea Butter Baby Album
Danity Kane- Damaged

Pop Smoke- Shoot For The Stars Aim For The Moon
Calvin Harris- Summer
Miley Cyrus- We Can't Stop, Party In The U.S.A,
Plastic Hearts, Prisoner, Angels Like You
Camila Cabello- Never Be the Same
Zara Larsson- Never Forget You
Cardi B – Bodak Yellow, Bartier Cardi, Press
Wolftyla- All Tinted, Play For Keeps
Jessie Reyez- Before Love Came to Kill Us
Kiana Lede- Second Chances, Mad at Me
Maroon 5 – She Will Be Loved
Nipsey Hussle- What It Feels Like
Dj Khaled- Wish Wish, Just Us, Celebrate

www.ingramcontent.com/pod-product-compliance
Lightning Source LLC
Chambersburg PA
CBHW021224090426
42740CB00006B/366